John Gilmary Shea, John Miller

A Description of the Province and City of New York

with plans of the city and several forts as they existed in the year 1695 -

Vol. 3

John Gilmary Shea, John Miller

A Description of the Province and City of New York
with plans of the city and several forts as they existed in the year 1695 - Vol. 3

ISBN/EAN: 9783337267711

Printed in Europe, USA, Canada, Australia, Japan

Cover: Foto ©Andreas Hilbeck / pixelio.de

More available books at **www.hansebooks.com**

A DESCRIPTION

OF

THE PROVINCE AND CITY

OF

NEW YORK;

WITH

PLANS OF THE CITY AND SEVERAL FORTS

AS THEY EXISTED IN THE YEAR 1695.

BY JOHN MILLER.

A NEW EDITION WITH AN INTRODUCTION AND COPIOUS HISTORICAL NOTES.

BY JOHN GILMARY SHEA, LL. D.,

MEMBER OF THE NEW YORK HISTORICAL SOCIETY.

> "Here lofty trees, to ancient song unknown,
> The noble sons of potent heat and floods,
> Prone-rushing from the clouds, rear high to Heaven
> Their thorny stems; and broad around them throw
> Meridian gloom. Here, in eternal prime,
> Unnumber'd fruits, of keen, delicious taste
> An I vital spirit, drink amid the cliffs,
> And burning sands that bank the shrubby vales."—THOMSON.

"It is from the bosom of colonies that civil liberty nearly in all ages has set forth; Greece had no Solon till the colonies of Asia Minor had attained their highest degree of splendor; and while the parent country could only boast of a single legislator, whose object was only to form citizens, and not merely warriors, nearly every colony of Greece and Sicily possessed its Zaleucus or Charondes. In this way indeed, every commercial state may be said to live again in the colonies it has founded. And though Europe should again experience the dreadful misfortune to sink under the yoke of despotism or anarchy, into the gloomy horrors of barbarism, Providence has provided for its re-birth, by scattering the seeds of civilization over every part of the globe; exhibiting in our day the astonishing spectacle, never before displayed, of ripened civilization in one part, while in others it is yet in blossom, or only pushing forth its earliest buds.". . . . . A. H. L. HEEREN.

NEW YORK:
WILLIAM GOWANS.

1862.

J. MUNSELL, PRINTER,
ALBANY.

DEDICATED

TO

THE MEMORY

OF

JOHN JAY.

ADVERTISEMENT.

The subscriber announces to the public, that he intends publishing a series of works, relating to the history, literature, biography, antiquities and curiosities of the Continent of America. To be entitled

GOWANS' BIBLIOTHECA AMERICANA.

The books to form this collection, will chiefly consist of reprints from old and scarce works, difficult to be produced in this country, and often also of very rare occurence in Europe; occasionally an original work will be introduced into the series, designed to throw light upon some obscure point of American history, or to elucidate the biography of some of the distinguished men of our land. Faithful reprints of every work published will be given to the public; nothing will be added, except in the way of notes, or introduction, which will be presented entirely distinct from the body of the work. They will be brought out in the best style, both as to the type, press work and paper, and in such a manner as to make them well worthy a place in any gentleman's library.

A part will appear about once every six months, or oftener, if the public taste demand it; each part forming an entire work, either an original production, or a reprint of some valuable, and at the same time scarce tract. From eight or twelve parts will form a handsome octavo volume, which the publisher is well assured, will be esteemed entitled to a high rank in every collection of American history and literature.

Should reasonable encouragement be given, the whole collection may in the course of no long period of time become not less voluminous, and quite as valuable to the student in American history, as the celebrated Harleian Miscellany is now to the student and lover of British historical antiquities.

W. GOWANS, *Publisher*.

INTRODUCTION.

The following description of the City and Colony of New York carries us back one hundred and sixty-six years to the day when William III ruled the destinies of the English nation. Its author, the Rev. John Miller, was for a time chaplain to the troops in the fort, and sole Episcopal clergyman in the colony. Beyond the account here given, and which he addressed to Henry Compton, Bishop of London, we have few data for his history. He was a graduate of one of the English universities, and was commissioned chaplain to two companies of Grenadiers in the Colony of New York, March 7, 1691-2. He arrived here in 1693, and as an act was passed that year for settling a ministry, he, in February, 1694, claimed a right to be inducted, but the Council decided against his pretensions. He left the colony apparently, June 1, 1695, and was taken in July by a French privateer, destroying his papers to avoid giving information to the enemy. His present account was therefore drawn up from recollection, and in fact is more taken up with a most extraordinary plan of civil and ecclesiastical government than with a detailed description of the colony in which he had sojourned. After his return to England he applied to the Commissioners of Trade and Plantation for additional salary, but did not succeed in obtaining anything. A short note of information furnished by him to the Board at the time is given in the Appendix.

Mr. Miller's Description, with its curious map and plans, found its way from the archives of the Bishops of London to the hands of George Chalmers the historian, and on the dispersion of his library fell into the hands of Thomas Rodd, a London bookseller, who published it in 1843. Since then the original manuscript has been added to the treasures in the British Museum.

Of Mr. Miller's earlier or later history I know nothing, and admit that I was deterred from seeking a clue for research by the slight results attained by Dr. O'Callaghan in his endeavors to investigate the history of Mr. Miller's predecessor in the chaplaincy, the Rev. Mr. Wolley. As connected with his history, however, we add his commission and the accompanying papers from the archives of the state.

New York at this period had just emerged from a civil war, that had been most disastrous to its prosperity. Submitting readily to the rule of William and Mary, it had seen the regular authorities overthrown by the ignorant and deluded or ambitious Leisler; whose sway, recognized in New York and on Long Island, was resisted at Albany, but who by stimulating the Iroquois to attack the French in Canada had contributed to the fearful slaughter of Lachine, and thus drawn on the exposed frontiers of New York the vengeance of the enemy, which soon laid Schenectady in ashes, and repeated on a diminished scale the horrors of Lachine. The terror inspired by this, the civil war existing and the oppressive measures of Leisler drove many from the colony, and it was fast declining, when Sloughter arrived, and his summary disposal of the usurper in turn made others deem flight a necessary precaution.

The Colony of New York had been the private property of James II as Duke of York, under the grant from his brother, and on his accession to the throne became an apanage of the crown, and subsequent monarchs so held it down to the close of the Revolution, when George III wished it to be so regarded.

During the period of James's actual possession of the territory, New York had been transformed into an English colony, a code of laws, compiled chiefly from those in force in New England, had been introduced, New York and Albany been incorporated, and finally a legislature assembled, which passed a bill of rights securing the liberties of the subject and granting free toleration to all Christians.

The acts of this legislature had been ignored by that convened under William III, and a resolution passed declaring them of no force. A new bill of rights, less generous indeed, was too full of dangerous ideas to meet the new champion of liberty, although it did not contain the "evil egg of toleration." The colony, when Miller came here, was divided into two parties, the Leislerian and Anti-Leislerian. Fletcher had identified himself with the latter, but the former had just succeeded in obtaining an act of parliament of a most false preamble, reversing the sentence on Leisler, and were to consummate their triumph by the king's appointment of Richard, Earl of Bellamont, as Governor, in place of Fletcher, whose extravagant grants of land afforded a good pretext for his removal.

New York city at this time was, as Miller's map shows, confined almost altogether to the part of the island below Wall street, where a palisade ran across the island, with stone bastions at Broadway and William street. A fort and a battery on the site of our present Battery, recently laid out by Fletcher, defended the city on the south, and other batteries and block houses on the river sides. The population was about four thousand, one-eighth being slaves. Yet the commerce was so considerable that in 1696, the year when Miller reached England, forty square-rigged vessels, sixty-two sloops, and as many boats, were entered at the New York custom house.

Bradford had just introduced printing in 1693, and in this very year, 1695, was printing the first New York Almanac for John Clapp, who is entitled to the honor of introducing hackney coaches into the city. A Dutch church had just been erected in Garden street, called Church street for that reason on Miller's map, although many a one yet remembers the time when it bore its earlier name. The Episcopalians were preparing to erect a church for themselves, and Miller advised the site of the bastion at the corner of Wall and William as the spot, but it was begun on the ground intended by Dongan for a Jesuit college, and next appropriated as a burial ground, the present site of Trinity.

New York possessed conveniences. It had its regular ferry to Brooklyn; its post to Philadelphia. Wells, to the number of a dozen, stood in the middle of the street in various parts and before the Fort, and the Stadt House, New York's first city hall, school house and court house. Provision was made for the prevention of fires, by leathern buckets, a system introduced in 1658, and of which at this time every house with three fireplaces was required to have two, brewers six, and bakers three, under penalty of a fine of six shillings.

Other improvements were talked of and introduced within a few years. Before the close of the century, Broad street was drained by a sewer, the residents on Broadway set out trees by consent of the Common Council, and every seventh house on the street hung out its lanthorn and candle on a pole, the expense of which was shared by all; Maiden lane and Garden street were laid out, a night watch of twelve men appointed, and a city livery of blue with orange list adopted.

In that day thirty volumes, including a couple of Bibles, was a large private library; and William Merritt, no friend to Leisler, was Mayor.

On the Hudson, Kingston, encircled with its palisade, was the chief place before you reached Albany, which then reached from Hudson street to Steuben on Broadway, and from the river west to Lodge street, where the old fort stood, Handlers' (that is Traders') street being the present Broadway. Dr. Dellius had his church commanding Broadway and Joncaer or State street, the fort being at the opposite end. Outside the city stockade were the Indian houses, where the Indians who came to trade or treat remained, and these were kept in repair at the expense of the traders.

The streets of Albany were not in very good condition, and the bridges, especially "the great bridge by Majr. Schuyler," was sadly out of repair, and the new stockades were not up; but the Common Council were taking steps to set all this right, removing houses too near the stockade, and digging a public well on Jonker street for the general good.

Albany had suffered greatly during the troubles, the number of men had fallen from 662 in 1689 to 382 in 1697, and the whole population from 2016 to 1449.

Schenectady had risen from its ruins, and now well defended was less fearful of a visitation.

Such was the colony as Miller left it, and his Description will bring it more fully before the reader. The moral tone was not what he desired, and he lays the lash on the prevalent vices with an unsparing hand. In his eyes the great want was the establishment of the Church of England, and his proposal of bishops is one of the earliest allusions to the step, which, natural and just wherever the Episcopalians were at all numerous, was strangely opposed by the people of New England, who insisted that their fellow Christians, the Episcopalians, should not have their church organization in America, and insisted so violently and intolerantly that many Episcopalians cowered under the storm of their fanaticism, and for peacesake endeavored to prevent any appointment. The Revolution alone freed the Episcopalians from this tyrannical interference of their neighbors. Had Miller's plan been set forward by Government, there might have been some pretext for their conduct.

Another theme of the Chaplain is the conquest of Canada; but here the same feeling of New England was shown towards the Catholics of Canada. They were not to profess or enjoy their religion at all. From the period of which we write to the year 1763 New England and New York sought the subjugation of Canada, mainly and chiefly to overthrow the Catholic religion. Miller's plan of extermination was thorough, and was doubtless that formed in the minds of most men in the northern colonies. Yet strange ordering of Providence, the blood of New England was poured out with this view, but left conquered Canada in the enjoyment of the religious liberty of which they wished to deprive her; and then the uprising against the Quebec act brought religious freedom at last to all the colonies, and the war which some consider as beginning with the attempt to prevent Episcopalians from having bishops beheld in its course the selectmen of Boston following vested Catholic clergymen through the streets, and soon after the close of the war, not only a bishop among the Episcopalians at Boston, but even one of the Catholics, and that one respected and beloved.

It will not be uninteresting to view the progress of New York from Miller's day to ours, and to give some picture of the city at present. To begin with the city, the following table will show its increase in population:

1696,....	4,302	1793,....	33,131	1835,....	270,068
1731,....	8,628	1800,....	60,489	1840,....	312,852
1756,....	10,381	1810,....	96,373	1850,....	515,394
1773,....	21,876	1823,....	123,706	1860,....	814,254
1786, ...	23,614	1830,....	202,589		

The whole population of the state in 1860 was 3,880,727, the city containing more than one-fifth of all the inhabitants of the state. The city has too, a greater population than Maine, New Hampshire, Vermont, Connecticut, Rhode Island, New Jersey, Michigan, Wisconsin, Iowa, Minnesota, Kansas, California, Oregon, Delaware, Maryland, Arkansas, Florida, South Carolina, Mississippi, Louisiana or Texas; twenty-one different states having a smaller population than has gathered on the island of Manhattan.

The appearance of the city has steadily improved. Scarcely a trace of the city of the days of the Revolution remains. The buildings are nearly all recent; the stores, many of them of white marble, brown stone or iron, are of palatial size and form; the churches and public edifices are equally costly and in many cases erected with great taste and judgment, possessing no little architectural beauty; what Wall street is for its banks, Broadway is for its stores and the Fifth avenue for its dwellings, the finest churches being in the last two streets or near them.

These various buildings are supplied with gas, first manufactured here in 1823, and with water from the Croton river, introduced in consequence of a vote in favor of it in 1835. The pavement of the streets has been gradually improved, the old cobble stones have given place in many parts to the Belgian pavement which has best answered the requisites; and the means of communication through the different parts are greatly facilitated by the various city rail roads. Steam brings to the city in the steam boats that leave at all points and in the various rail roads her supplies and merchandise; and drives the machinery in her thousand workshops; and even in her fire engines bends its immense strength to hurl the exhaustless Croton on the consuming edifice.

For education New York possesses, including the Free Academy, five incorporated colleges, and ninety-nine public schools, besides a large number directed by private individuals or religious denominations. The pupils in the public schools amount to over fifty thousand, and nearly fifteen thousand more are taught in other free schools. Her public libraries, the Astor, Society, Historical, Mercantile and others, though inferior to the great libraries of Europe, are rapidly meeting the wants of the people.

In her institutions for the relief of the miseries and misfortunes of our race, New York has no reason to avoid comparison. Two well conducted city hospitals, three more supported by the Catholics, Jews and Episcopalians; several orphan asylums, infirmaries, asylums for the blind, the deaf and dumb, and the insane, a Lying-in Hospital, houses of protection for servants. In addition to these it has an institution not indeed a charity, for the city contributes nothing to it, but no less admirable, as it is managed by citizens of New York. This is the Emigrant Commission, supported by a tax levied on each emigrant arriving, and paid by him as a premium insuring him in case of want during five years a competent relief. Of the magnitude of this institution, we may judge by the fact that from 1847 to 1861 the number of emigrants landing at New York was over two million seven hundred and fifty thousand, and of this great nation not one during the five years succeeding his arrival cost the city or any part of the state a single cent.

The Alms House of the city, with the Penitentiary, the Juvenile Asylums, are all extensive, and generally conducted on wise principles, the government devolving chiefly on a single Board of Charities and Corrections.

Meanwhile the city has its numerous churches and edifices growing out of them; its convents, asylums, hospitals. Many of the churches are large and spacious, with costly organs and rich service; most are well attended by worshipers, some by four or five times their capacity each Sunday, repeated services at different hours enabling thousands to use a single edifice.

While religion and benevolence are thus cared for, New York is not without its means of amusement. A spacious park of three miles length, has been laid out most economically in a period of official squandering, and by its walks and drives, its sailing advantages in summer and still greater opportunities for skating in winter, gives a guarantee of the public health, which the improved sewerage and widening of many streets in the older parts of the city daily insures. A noble Opera House, and a number of Theatres, a Museum, attract numbers, and the amusements offered are watched with a jealous eye. At no period, perhaps, has greater morality marked the plays selected for the stage.

Such in brief is New York in 1862, how altered from

that when Miller made his notes. The rocky isle alone preserves its identity. The picture of the past, therefore, possesses but the greater interest.

Commission of the Rev. John Miller to be Chaplain of Fort William, New York.

From Book of Commissions II, 71-73 in Secretary's Office, Albany, N. Y.

Marie R.

[L. S.] William and Mary by the grace of God King and Queen of England Scotland ffrance and Ireland Defenders of the faith &c. To our Trusty and welbeloved John Miller Clerke Greeting We do by these presents constitute and appoint you to be Chaplain of the two Companies of foot in the Colony of Newyorke in America You are therefore carefully and diligently to discharge the duty of a Chaplain by doing and performing all and all manner of things thereunto belonging and you are to observe and follow such orders and direccons from time to time as you shall receive from your Captains or any your superiour Officer according to the rules and discipline of warr Given at Our Court at Whitehall the 7th day of March 169½ in the fourth yeare of Our Reigne By her Maj^{tys} Command

NOTTINGHAM.

Entered with the Com^r Genl of the musters.

D. CRAWFORD.

The Bishop of London's Licence to the Revd John Miller.

[L. S.] Henricus permissione divina Londinensis Episcopus Dilecto nobis in Christo Johannis Miller Art: Magistro & Clerico Salutem & Gratiam Ad peragendum Officium Capellani in Oppido Novi Eboraci apud Americanos in precibus communibus Aliisq ; ministerijs Ecclesiasticis Ad Officium Capellani pertinentibus juxta formam descriptam in libro publicarum precum authoritate Parliamenti hujus Inclyti Regni Angliæ in ea parte edit. & provis. & Canones & Constitutiones in ea legitime stabilitas et publicatas non aliter neque alio modo Tibi de cujus fidelitate, morum integritate Literarum Scientia sana doctrina et diligentia plurimum confidimus (prestito primitus per te Juramento tam de agnoscendo Regiam supremam Majestatem juxta vim formam et effectum Statuti parliamenti dicti reg- [III. London] ni Angliæ in ea parte edit. et provis. quam de Canonica Obedientia Nobis et Successoribus nostris in omnibus licitis et honestis per te præstanda et exhibenda, subscriptisq ; per te tribus illis articulis mentionatis in tricesimo sexto Capitulo libri Constitutionum sive Canonum Ecclesiasticorum Anno Dom. 1604. Regia Authoritate Editorum & promulgatorum) Licentiam et facultatem nostram concedimus et impertimur per præsentes ad nostrum beneplacitum duntaxat duraturas : In cujus rei Testimonium Sigillum nostrum (quo in similibus plerumq; utimur) præsentibus apponi fecimus Dat. nono die Martij Anno Dom. 1691, nostræq translationis anno Decimo Septimo.

Certificate of the Rev^l Mr Miller having subscribed the Declaration according to Act of Parliament.

[L. S.] Henry, By Divine permission Lord Bishop of London to all to whom these presents shall or may concerne health in Our Lord God everlasting. Whereas by virtue of An Act of Parliament made in the first year of the reign of Our Sovereign Lord and Lady King William and Queen Mary Entituled an Act for the abrogating of the Oaths of Supremacy and Allegiance and appointing other oaths It is provided and Enacted That every person at his or their respective Admission to be incumbent in any Ecclesiasticall promotion or dignity in the Church of England shall subscribe and declare before his Ordinary in manner and forme as in the said Act is contained Now know ye That on the day of the date hereof did personally [H London] appear before us Mr John Miller Clerke to be admitted Chaplain in Newyorke in America and subscribed as followeth as by the said Act is required : " I John Miller Clerke do declare that no forrein Prince Person Prelate State or Potentate hath or ought to have any Jurisdiction Power Superiority Preëminence or Authority Ecclesiasticall or Spiritual within this Realm: And that I will conform to the Liturgy of the Church of England as it is now by Law Established" In Witness whereof We have caused Our Seal Manual to be affixed to these presents Dated the 9th day of March in the year of Our Lord One thousand six hundred 91 And in the 17th Year of Our Translation.

A
Description
OF
The Province and City
OF
New-York:

With

Plans of the City and Several Forts
as they exifted in the Year 1695.

By the

Rev. John Miller.

LONDON,

Printed and Publifhed for the Enlightment of
fuch as would defire information Anent the New-
Found-Land of America.

ADVERTISEMENT

TO THE ENGLISH EDITION.

THE following description of New York, as it existed a century and a half since, fell into the hands of the publisher on the dispersion of the library of the late George Chalmers, Esq.

As it contains some curious particulars respecting the state of society in the province at the time, and is, moreover, of particular local interest, as giving plans of the town and the several forts in the province, the publisher thought he would be rendering an acceptable service to those persons who take an interest in tracing the rise and growth of the great commercial emporium of the Western world by causing a few copies to be printed, and thus preserving it from the chance of being lost or destroyed.

The orthography has been modernized, the pointing amended, and a few words, obviously necessary to complete the sense, have been inserted between brackets.

The author appears to use some peculiar arithmetical notation consisting in the employment of a superfluous number of ciphers, as page 5, line 4, where 300 and 303 are printed for 30 and 33, and page 14, where 64,000 is used for 64: these are retained, but his obvious meaning is indicated to the reader by inserting the true numbers within a parenthesis.

It may be further necessary to add, that the author uniformly uses Canida instead of Canada: this has been changed to the present usage. All other proper names are given as in the manuscript.

*To the Right Reverend Father in God, Henry,
Lord Bishop of London.*

MY LORD.

AFTER having been very near three years resident in the province of New York, in America, as Chaplain to his Majesty's forces there, and by living in the Fort of New York, and constantly attending the Governor, had the opportunity of observing many things of considerable consequence in relation to the Christians and Indians, inhabitants thereof, or bordering thereon, and also taken the draughts of all the cities, towns, forts, and churches of any note within the same, with particular accounts of the number of our Indians, the strength of Canada, and way thither, and several other matters which would have enabled me to give an exact account of the present estate of that province and the methods proper to be used for the correcting certain evils therein, and advantaging thereof, principally as to religious affairs,—I was (obliged so to do by several weighty motives, especially those of my private concerns) returning home with them in July last, when being met and set upon by a French privateer and made his prisoner, I was obliged to cause them all to be thrown overboard, lest I should have given intelligence to an enemy to the ruine of the province, instead of a friendly information to the advantaging thereof. But having had time by my long imprisonment, and leisure also sufficient, I thought I could not better employ them than by endeavouring to retrieve some part of what I had lost, and put it in such a method as might testify the earnest desire I have to promote the glory to God, the service of my sovereign, and the benefit of my country. What I have been able to do through God's assistance, the help of my memory, and certain knowledge I had of things, your Lordship will find in the following sheets: which however weak and imperfect, as it must needs be, I humbly present to your Lordship as an evidence of my duty and gratitude; submitting it to your wise inspection and serious consideration, either to be further improved if it seem proper for the end it is designed, or rejected if it be unworthy of any respect. Intreating your Lordship to pardon what faults and blemishes shall be found therein, and heartily praying that the Giver of all good things would bless your Lordship, (see Note 1,) with health, and prosperity and success in all your affairs, I make bold in all duty to subscribe myself,

   My Lord,
    Your Lordship's most faithful,
      And humble servant,
        JOHN MILLER.

NEW YORK CONSIDERED.

CHAPTER I.

OF THE PROVINCE OF NEW YORK.

The province of New York is a country very pleasant and delightful, and well improved for the time it has been settled and the number of its inhabitants. It lies in the latitudes of 40 and 41, and for the longitude is situated between the 300th and 303d (30th and 33d) degree north; is in breadth, where broadest, from the east to the west, about 200 miles, and in length, north and south, about 250, being bounded on the east by New England, on the west by New Jersey and the Indian country, on the north by the Indian country, and on the south by the ocean. It lies almost exactly in the middle of the English plantations, which altogether have of sea coast, more or less improved by the English, both eastward and westward, near 250 leagues. This province whereof I speak consists partly of islands and partly of the main land: the islands of greater consideration are three: New York island,

Staten Island, and Nassau (formerly Long) Island; (see Note 2,) the two former make, each of them, a county, the first of New York, the second of Richmond. On Nassau Island are three counties; for the western end is King's County, the middle Queen's County, and the eastern part Suffolk County: to these do belong several other smaller islands, which, being at best but so many farms, are not worthy consideration. On the main land are likewise five counties, namely: West Chester, Orange, Dutchess, Ulster, and Albany, (see Note 3,) equal in number to, but not so well planted, improved, and peopled, as the former. The places of strength are chiefly three: the city of New York, the city of Albany, and the town of Kingstone, in Ulster.

The city of New York, more largely taken, is the whole island so called, and is in length sixteen miles, (see Note 4,) in breadth six, and in circumference forty-two; but more strictly considered, and as a place of strength, is only the part thereof within the fortifications, and so is not in length or breadth above two furlongs, and in circumference a mile. The form of it is triangular, having for the sides thereof the west and north lines, and the east and south for its arched basis. The chief place of strength it boasts of is its fort, situated on the south west angle, which is reasonably strong, and well provided with ammunition, having in it about thirty-eight guns. Mounted on the basis likewise, in convenient places, are three batteries of great guns; one of fifteen, called Whitehall Battery, one of five, by the Stadthouse, (see Note 5,) and the third of ten, by the Burgher's Path. (See Note 6.) On the north east angle is a strong blockhouse and half moon, wherein are six or seven guns; this part buts upon the river, and is all along fortified with a sufficient bank of earth. On the north side are two large stone points, and therein about eight guns, some mounted and some unmounted. On the north west angle is a blockhouse, and on the west side two hornworks which are furnished with some guns, six or seven in number: this side buts upon Hudson's River; has a bank in some places twenty fathoms high from the water, by reason whereof, and a stockado strengthened with a bank of earth on the inside, which last is also on the north side to the landward, it is not easily assailable. As this city is the chief place of strength belonging to this province for its defence against those enemies who come by sea, so Albany is of principal consideration against those who come by land, the French and Indians of Canada. It is distant from New York 150 miles, and lies up Hudson's River on the west side, on the descent of a hill from the west to the eastward. It is in circumference about six furlongs, and hath therein about 200 houses, a fourth part of what there is reckoned to be in New York. The form of it is septangular, and the longest line that which buts upon the river running from the north to the south. On the west angle is the fort, quadrangular, strongly stockadoed and ditched round, having in it twenty-one pieces of ordnance mounted. On the north west side are two blockhouses, and on the south west as many: on the south east angle stands one blockhouse; in the middle of the line from thence northward is a horned work, and on the north east angle a mount. The whole city is well stockadoed round, and in the several fortifications named are about thirty guns. Dependent on this city, and about twenty miles distance to the northward from it, is the Fort of Scanectade, (see Note 7,) quadrangular, with a treble stockado, a new blockhouse at every angle, and in each blockhouse two great guns; and Nestigayuna, and the Half-moon; (see Note 8,) places, formerly of some account, but now deserted. On this city also depends the Fort at the Flats, four miles from Albany, belonging to the River Indians, who are about sixty families: it is stockadoed round, has a blockhouse and a mount, but no great guns. There are in it five Indian wigwams, and a house or two serving in case of necessity for the soldiers, in number twenty-four, who are the guard there. Kingstone is the chief town of Ulster County; lies on the west side of Hudson's River, but two miles distant from it, from New York eighty-six, and from Albany sixty-four miles: it is quadrangular, and stockadoed round, having small hornworks at convenient distances one from the other, and in proper places. It is in circumference near as big as Albany, but as to number of houses not above half so big: on the south side is a particular part separated by a stockado from the rest, and strengthened with a blockhouse and a hornwork wherein are about six guns.

The number of the inhabitants in this province are about 3000 families, whereof almost one-half are naturally Dutch, a great part English, and the rest French; which how they are seated, and what number of families of each nations, what churches, meeting houses, ministers or pretended ministers, there are in each county, may be best discerned by the table here inserted. As to their religion, they are very much divided; few of them intelligent and sincere, but the most part ignorant and conceited, fickle and regardless. As to their wealth and disposition thereto, the Dutch are rich and sparing; the English neither very rich, nor too great husbands; the French are poor, and therefore forced to be penurious. As to their way of trade and dealing, they are all generally cunning and crafty, but many of them not so just to their words as they should be.

The air of this province is very good, and much like that of the best parts of France; not very often foggy, nor yet cloudy or rainy for any long time together, but generally very clear and thin: the north-west winds frequently visit it, and chiefly in winter; nor does there want in the summer the southern breezes, which daily almost rise about nine or ten in the morning, and continue till sunset. The weather is, indeed, hotter in summer than one would well wish it, and in winter colder than he can well endure it; but both heat and cold are in their seasons much abated by the wind last spoken of. The coldest wind is generally reckoned to be the north west, and it is certainly very sharp and piercing, and causes most hard and severe frosts; but, in my judgment, the south west exceeds it much, but the best of it is that it does not blow very often there from that quarter.

The air and winds being such as I have said, the country, consequently, should be very healthful, and this is certainly so; and I dare boldly affirm it to be, on that particular and most beneficial account, the best province his Majesty has in all America, and very agreeable to the constitution of his subjects, so that a sober Englishman may go into it, live there, and come out of it again, without any seasoning or other sickness caused merely by the country; nay, it is so far from causing, that, on the contrary, if a man be any thing consumptive, and not too far gone, 'tis ten to one but it will cure him; and if inclined to rheums or colds, will in a great part, if not wholly, free him from them.

If the air be good, the land is not bad, but taking one place with another, very tolerable, yea, commendable: there are, 'tis true, many rocks and mountains, but, I believe, the goodness of their inside as to metals and minerals will, when searched, make amends for the barrenness of the outside: there are also many woods and bogs, or rather swamps; but few complain of them, because they afford them mast for their hogs and food for their breeding mares and cows, also, in the summer time, fur. Walnut, cedar, oak of several kinds, and many other sorts of wood proper for building of ships or houses, or necessary for fencing and fuel; turpentine for physical uses, and pitch and tar for the seaman's service; many physical herbs, and much wild fowl, as swans, geese, ducks, turkies, a kind of pheasants and partridges, pigeons, &c. and no less store of good venison, so that you may sometimes buy at your door a quarter for ninepence or a shilling. Hence also they have their furs, such as beaver, otter, fisher, martin, musk-rat, bearskin, &c. Indeed, the countenance of them is not so beautiful as some of our English writers would make us believe; nor would I prefer, in that respect, the wild Indian country before our English meadows and closes, much less our gardens when in the most flourishing estate, notwithstanding that there are here and there many herbs such and as good as we have growing in our gardens to be found wild, as mint, sweet marjoram, &c.; and, in their season, strawberries and walnuts and some other sorts of fruits, in great abundance, especially grapes, which I am persuaded, if well improved, would yield great quantities of strong and pleasant wine (see Note 9).

He that is not pleased with these advantages may, if he please to take a little pains in clearing the ground by stubbing up the trees and brushwood, have good arable land or pastures, that shall, instead of woods and their wild produce, afford him good corn and hay, and a reasonable number of fat cattle. Indeed, not all alike, for the land toward the south is generally a sandy soil, and not very fruitful, but rather something inclining to barrenness: the corn that it produces is small, oftentimes spoiled by blasts and mildews, or eaten (especially the white peas,) by the worms, but then it produces very good Indian corn or maize; (see Note 10,) pleasant fruits, as apples, peaches, melons of several sorts; good roots as parsneps, turnips, carrots, and as good cabbages as need to be eaten: but to the northward, and in the Indian country, the land is much better; the soil black and rich, brings forth corn in abundance, and that very firm, large, and good; and besides all those fruits aforementioned (peaches excepted), cherries, pears, and currants.

Fish there is in great store, both in the sea and rivers; many of them of the same kinds as we have in England, and many strange, and such as are not to be seen there; some even without name, except such as was given them from the order they were taken in, as first, second, third, &c., (see Note 11). These are the produce of the country I speak of, and there are yet more than these peculiarly proper for the merchant, as train oil and whalebone, though in no very great quantity; and pipe-staves, of which many thousands are yearly transported, with several other things, which, with some of those before-named, will admit of much improvement. The industry that now is used is but little; the few inhabitants, having a large country before them, care not for more than from hand to mouth, and therefore they take but little pains, and yet that little produces very good beer, bread, cider, wine of peaches, cloth stuffs, and beaver hats, a certain and sufficient sign how plentiful and beneficial a country it would be did but industrious art second nature's bounty, and were but the inhabitants more in number than at present they are (see Note 12).

Merchandizing in this country is a good employment, English goods yielding in New York generally 100 per cent. advance above the first cost, and some of them 200, 300, yea sometimes 400: this makes so many in the city to follow it, that whosoever looks on their shops would wonder, where there are so many to sell, there should be any to buy.

This, joined to the healthfulness, pleasantness, and fruitfulness thereof, are great encouragements to people rather to seek the bettering of their fortunes here than elsewhere; so that it may be hoped that a little time will render the inhabitants more

numerous than at present they are. Do men
expect profit in what they carry with them to a
foreign land?—they need not fear it here, if their
goods but suit the country. Would they live in
health?—no place so likely to live so in, in this
part of America. Would they have plenty of neces-
saries for food and raiment?—New York, in these,
is not unkind; but though a stepmother to those
who come from England, yet furnishes them as
plentifully, if equally industrious, as their natural
country does those who stay behind. In short,
there is nothing wanting to make the inhabitants
thereof happy but some things which the country
cannot help them in, nor yet is guilty of the
want thereof, to which either themselves do con-
tribute, or which their ill settlement, or worse government, has introduced, and some things which
the few years of their being a province has not yet
given any favorable opportunities for, nor permitted
to be settled among them; which what they are
I shall next proceed to discover and speak of in
the best method and order that I can, and with as
much brevity as the subject will conveniently admit
of, after having first presented to the reader some
draughts or ground plots of the most remarkable
places already discoursed of, as you will perceive
by considering these following figures:—

NEW YORK IN 1695.

COUNTIES.	CHURCHES.	MINISTERS.	FAMILIES.
NEW YORK.	Chapel in the fort Dutch Calvinists Dutch Lutheran French Jews Synagogue Haarlem	Dr. Selinus (See Note 13.) Dr. Perot (See Note 14.) Saul Brown (See Note 15.) Dr. Selinus	90 150 30 200 20 25 English 40, Dissenters.
RICHMOND.	A Meeting House	Dr. Bonrepos (See 16.)	English 40 Dutch 44 French 36
KING'S.	Flatbush Utrecht Brookland	Dr. Varick died Aug. 1694, and another sent for May 27, 1695.	300 or 400, chiefly Dutch.
QUEEN'S.	Jamaica Hampsted } Meeting Houses Newtown	Mr. Philips) without Mr. Vesey* } any Mr. Mott†) orders.	300 or 400 English, most Dissenters, and some Dutch.
SUFFOLK.	Eight or nine Meeting Houses; almost one at every town.	Seven Ministers, Dissenters, Presbyterian, or Independent. One lately gone to Scotland.	500 or 600 English, and Dissenters for the most part.
WEST CHESTER.	A Meeting House at West Chester.	A young man coming to settle there without any orders. (See Note 19.)	200 or 300 English and Dissenters; few Dutch.
ORANGE.			20 English & Dutch.
DUTCHESS.			30 English & Dutch.
ULSTER.	Dutch Calvinist, at Kingstone, for five or six towns.	A Minister to come, his books brought; but he missed his passage.	300, Dutch mostly; some English and French.
ALBANY.	Dutch Calvinist Dutch Lutheran Scanecthade Kinderhoeck.	Dr. Dellius. (See Note 20.) A Dutch Minister sent for.	400 or 500 Dutch, all Calvinists, except 12 or 14 Lutherans.

* See Note 17.   † See Note 18.

CHAPTER II.

OF THE EVILS AND INCONVENIENCES IN NEW YORK.

Come we now to consider those things which I have said to be either wanting or obstructive to the happiness of New York; and here I shall not speak of every slight and trivial matter, but only those of more considerable importance, which I count to be six. 1st, The wickedness and irreligion of the inhabitants; 2d, want of ministers; 3d, difference of opinion in religion; 4th, a civil dissension; 5th, the heathenism of the Indians; and, 6th, the neighborhood of Canada: of every one of these I shall say something as shall be most material.

The first is the wickedness and irreligion of the inhabitants, which abounds in all parts of the province, and appears in so many shapes, constituting so many sorts of sin, that I can scarce tell which to begin withal. But, as a great reason of and inlet to the rest, I shall first mention the great negligence of divine things that is generally found in most people, of what sect or party soever they pretend to be: their eternal interests are their least concern, and, as if salvation were not a matter of moment, when they have opportunities of serving God they care not for making use thereof; or, if they go to church, 'tis but too often out of curiosity, and to find out faults in him that preacheth rather than to hear their own, or, what is yet worse, to slight and deride where they should be serious. If they have none of those opportunities, they are well contented, and regard it little if there be any who seem otherwise and discontented. Many of them, when they have them, make appear by their actions 'twas but in show; for though at first they will pretend to have a great regard for God's ordinances, and a high esteem for the ministry, whether real or pretended, a little time will plainly evidence that they were more pleased at the novelty than truly affected with the benefit, when they slight that which they before seemingly so much admired, and speak evil of him who before was the subject of their praise and commendation, and that without any other reason than their own fickle temper and envious humour. In a soil so rank as this, no marvel if the Evil One find a ready entertainment for the seed he is minded to cast in; and from a people so inconstant, and regardless of heaven and holy things, no wonder if God withdraw his grace, and give them up a prey to those temptations which they so industriously seek to embrace: hence is it, therefore, that their natural corruption without check or hinderance is, by frequent acts, improved into habits most evil in the practice, and difficult in the correction.

One of which, and the first I am minded to speak, of, is drunkenness, which, though of itself a great sin, is yet aggravated in that it is an occasion of many others. 'Tis in this country a common thing, even for the meanest persons, so soon as the bounty of God has furnished them with a plentiful crop, to turn what they can as soon as may be into money, and that money into drink, at the same time when their family at home have nothing but rags to protect their bodies from the winter's cold; nay if the fruits of their plantations be such as by their own immediate labour convertible into liquor, such as cider, perry, &c., they have scarce the patience to stay till it is fit for drinking, but, inviting their pot-companions, they all of them, neglecting whatsoever work they are about, set to it together, and give not over till they have drunk it off. And to these sottish engagements they will make nothing to ride ten or twenty miles, and at the conclusion of one debauch another generally is appointed, except their stock of liquor fail them. Nor are the mean and country people only guilty of this vice, but they are equalled, nay surpassed, by many in the city of New York, whose daily practice is to frequent the taverns, and to carouse and game their night employment. This course is the ruin and destruction of many merchants, especially those of the younger sort, who, carrying over with them a stock, whether as factors, or on their own account, spend, even to prodigality, till they find themselves bankrupt ere they are aware (see Note 21).

In a town where this course of life is led by

many, 'tis no wonder if there be other vices in vogue, because they are the natural product of it, such are cursing and swearing, to both of which people are here much accustomed; some doing it in that frequent, horrible, and dreadful manner as if they prided themselves both as to the number and invention of them: this, joined with their profane, atheistical and scoffing method of discourse, makes their company extremely uneasy to sober and religious men, who sometimes, by reason of their affairs, cannot help being of their society, and becoming ear-witnesses of their blasphemy and folly. 'Tis strange that men should engage themselves so foolishly, and run into the commission of so great a sin unto which they have no sufficient, often not a pretended, provocation, and from which they reap no advantage nor any real pleasure: and yet we see them even delight in it, and no discourse is thought witty or eloquent except larded with oaths and execrations. Howsoever difficult these sins may be to be corrected in a large and populous kingdom, I should scarce think them so in a province, where the total number of inhabitants will scarce equal the 64,-000th (64th) part of those who are computed to be in London; nay, am sure they might be much hindered, were but the good laws made against them put duly in execution.

'Tis an ordinary thing with vices that one of them introduces another, and is a reason of their easy and common success; and so we see it here. That where men drink to so high a pitch, and pamper their debauched palates with the rich and most nourishing viands the country affords, 'tis certain the flesh must grow high and rebellious, so as imperiously to command where it ought to obey; nay, not to be contented without variety, whatsoever obstacle or impediment lies in the way. Reason, that should rule and direct to better things, is so far debauched, that she pretends to defend the contrary; and by objecting the troubles and confinements of a married state, and extolling the sweet and unconfined pleasures of the wandering libertines, prevails with many not to think fornication, nay, not adultery, dangerous sins, but rather to be chosen than lawful wedlock, the proper and really sufficient (though not to debauched and pampered bodies) remedy for the hinderance of these evils. I say it is a proper and sufficient remedy if duly practiced, and according to law and reason, which in New York it is not; because,

1st. There are many couples live together without ever being married in any manner of way; many of whom, after they have lived some years so, quarrel, and, thereupon separating, take unto themselves, either in New York or some other province, new companions; but, grant they do not so, how can such expect that God should bless them together while they live in open contempt of his holy ordinance?

2d. Those who in earnest do intend to be married together are in so much haste, that, commonly, enjoyment precedes the marriage, to which they seldom come till a great belly puts it so forward, that they must either submit to that, or to shame and disgrace which they avoid by marriage; ante-nuptial fornication, where that succeeds, being not looked upon as any scandal or sin at all.

3d. There is no sufficient provision for the marrying of people in this province, the most that are married here being married by justices of the peace, for which there neither is nor can be in New York any law: (see Note 22,) on this account, many looking upon it as no marriage at all, and being easily induced to think it so when they find themselves pinched by the contract, think it no great matter to divorce themselves, as they term it, and marry to others where they can best, and according to their own liking. Whether this manner of marrying by justices of the peace be a sufficient engagement to the married couple to live together, is to me a matter not disputable; and, in the meanwhile, the scandal and evil that flows from hence is very great: and I myself know at this time a man who fills the place and exercises the office of a minister and school-master in the island of Barbadoes that was married to a woman of New York by a justice of peace, and, after falling out with her, betook himself to another woman, whom he got with child, and went afterwards to Barbadoes, where, if he be not married to her, at least he lives with her as though she were his wife; the woman the meantime continuing in New York, was soon after married to another man.

4th. Supposing the way of marrying were lawful, yet many justices are so ignorant or mean-spirited, or both, that thereby it comes to pass they are often prevailed upon to marry a couple together that are either one or both of them engaged or married to other persons: an eminent instance hereof I knew in New York. A woman, dissolute in manners, not liking to live with her husband, contracted herself to another person, and came with him to a justice of peace to be married. The justice, knowing the woman to be the wife of another man, refused at first to marry them; but they, understanding he had offended in the like matter before, threatened to acquaint the Governor therewith, if he would not marry them also; which rather than hazard, he granted their request; thus offending the first time through ignorance, and the second through fear I came to know of it by this means:—the woman thus married outliving her second husband, had inveigled the son of an honest woman of Nassau Island to marry her, her first husband still living: his mother, looking upon such a match as his ruin, sought all she could to hinder it, and, as her last refuge, came to me, desiring me to do what I could that he might not have a license out of the Secretary's office, which I obstructed by entering a caveat, and so prevented it for that time; and what is done in it since I cannot tell: but this am sure of, that the too frequent practice of this evil is such as loudly calls for redress and amendment.

The great encouragement for gaining a livelihood that is given to people in this province, where whosoever will take pains may have land enough whereon to raise an estate for themselves and heirs, and the mean accommodations or at least the no great riches, of the first inhabitants, have been the reason that thieving and robbing has been very little practised in this country. But now, of late, since some people are become wealthy enough to purchase and have by them what is worth the taking away, and that the out-parts of the province (where the best land is) towards Canada are so harassed by the French and their Indians, that men are fearful to plant and dwell there, and that people are fallen into so great debauchery and idleness, thieving is become more frequent; and many considerable robberies have been committed in my time in New York, to the great discouragement of industrious people, and increase of vice and sin. There are many other wickednesses which I might speak of as wanting redress, but there is no need of enlarging on their account; for, were these of greater note already spoken of discouraged, the rest would of themselves fall to nothing.

CHAPTER III.

OF THE MINISTRY, AND DEFICIENCY THEREIN.

A second and great inconveniency this province suffers under is in relation to a ministry; for it is most certain, that where there are persons of some repute and authority living, who give good example by their sober lives and conversations, and diligence in their duty, sin is mightily discouraged, and religion and virtue gain ground upon her daily, and increase and flourish; and that, where there are none such, vice has a free course, and religion continually decays, and, what by the negligence of men, and the malice and subtility of the enemy of all, goodness runs to ruin. Now, in New York, there are either

1, No ministers at all, that is, the settled and established religion of the nation, and of such there is not, oftentimes, one in the whole province; nor at any time, except the Chaplain to his Majesty's forces in New York, (see Note 23,) that does discharge, or pretend to discharge, the duty of a minister, and, he being but one, cannot do it everywhere; nay, but in very few places but New York itself: and being necessitated sometimes to go to England, it happens that both the garrison and the city are without a minister a year together. It happens, also, that he is often changed, which is not without its inconveniences, but proves very prejudicial to religion in many cases, as is easy to instance: besides, while he does his duty among them, he shall experience their gratitude but very little, and be sure to meet with a great many discouragements, except, instead of reprehending and correcting, he will connive at and soothe people in their sinful courses.

2, Or secondly, if there be any ministers, they are such as only call themselves so, and are but pretended ministers; many of them have no orders at all, but set up for themselves of their own head and authority; or, if they have orders, are Presbyterians, Independents, &c. Now all these have no other encouragement for the pains they pretend to take than the voluntary contributions of the people, or, at best, a salary by agreement and subscription, which yet they shall not enjoy, except they take more care to please the humours and delight the fancies of their hearers, than to preach up true religion and a christian life: hence it comes to pass that the people live very loosely, and they themselves very poorly, at best, if they are not forced for very necessity, and by the malice of some of their hearers, to forsake their congregations. Besides being of different persuasions, and striving to settle such sentiments as they indulge themselves in in the hearts of those who are under their ministry, they do more harm, in distracting and dividing the people, than good in the amending their lives and conversations.

3, Or thirdly, if there be, or have been any ministers, and those ministers of the Church of England, they have been here, and are in other provinces, many of them, such as, being of a vicious life and conversation, have played so many vile pranks, and shewn such an ill light, as has been very prejudicial to religion in general, and the Church of England in particular; or else they have been such as, though sober, yet have been very young, and so, instead of doing good, have been easily drawn into the commission of evil, and become as scandalous as those last mentioned. Now though, as to this last charge, I must not be conceived to speak so much in relation to New York as the other English plantations, because there has been generally, from time to time, but one minister at a time as Chaplain to his Majesties forces there, yet is not New York wholly unconcerned herein, since, there having been several chaplains successive to one another, some have not so carried themselves as to be, and that deservedly, without blame: besides, three that I know of have come by the by, whose either life or knowledge, or both, have not been commendable; and, as I am informed, there is one there now, and another going from Barbadoes, the former not free from all exception, and the latter lying under very great scandal.

CHAPTER IV.

OF DIFFERENCE IN RELIGION.

The province of New York being peopled by several nations, there are manifold and different opinions of religion among them; as to which, though there are but very few of any sect who are either real or intelligent, yet several of the partizans of each sort have every one such a desire of being uppermost, and increasing the number of their own party, that they not only thereby make themselves unhappy by destroying true piety, and setting up instead thereof a fond heat and blind zeal for they know not what, but also industriously obstruct the settlement of the established religion of the nation, which only can make them happy; and have hitherto, either by their craft and cunning, or their money, prospered in their designs; and to do thus they have but too much pretence, from the scandalous lives of some ministers—the matter considered under the former head.

CHAPTER V.

OF THE CIVIL DIVISION.

I shall, in the fourth place, reckon as not a small unhappiness to the province of New York the division in the civil state happening on this occasion. When his present gracious Majesty came into England to redeem us from Popery and arbitrary power, the news of his success arriving in New England, put some people there upon overturning the government, which they affected: how just their reasons and proceedings were is not my business to inquire, but this action of theirs put the inhabitants of New York upon the like project. Colonel Nicholson, the then Lieutenant Governor, and the council, thought it best to attend orders what they should do from England; and in the meanwhile, the Colonel, to free the people from all jealousies and fears, permitted daily a proportionable part of the city train-bands to have the guard of the fort with the King's soldiers. But Mr. Jacob Leysler, a man of small beginnings, but thence grown a merchant, and about this time decaying in his fortune, and others of his party, were no ways contented with this moderate course proposed, but, pretending fears of being sold or given to the French, and terming all Papists, or popishly affected, who did not favor his designs, seized upon the fort and government too, in the management of which he did many good things; and, if people say truth, was guilty of doing many things that were irregular, and some very bad, as unlawfully imprisoning the King's subjects, taking away their goods by force, designing to kill the natural English and all who joined with them, man, woman, and child, &c.; so that when Colonel Slaughter came over in March 1691, he and one Mr. Milburn his son-in-law, who had greatly counselled and assisted him in his designs, were tried for their lives and condemned, and, what is more, hanged, to the great sorrow and regret of their whole party, who have vowed revenge, and, some say, want but an opportunity to effect their purpose. I shall not pretend here to enquire into the real intentions or actions of Leysler's party, or those who were against them, neither into the truth of those things which the one party allege against the other; but only say, that, having considered what I have seen done and heard said on the one side and on the other, I do believe that there were some of either side who sought in what they did their own advantage; many who truly did intend his Majesty's service; and many who blindly followed the leading men, neither considering what they did, nor whether they led them; and that these injuries, done by either side to their opposites, have made a most unhappy division and breach among them, which will hardly of a long time admit of cure, except some very prudent and moderate method be used for that purpose more than has already been put in practice (see Note 24).

CHAPTER VI.

OF THE HEATHENISM OF THE INDIANS.

The next thing in this province blameable is the heathenism of the natural Indians, who here, in the very heart of a Christian country, practice their barbarous and devilish customs and modes of worship, notwithstanding it is now sixty years and more since Christians first inhabited this country, and thirty years since the English were possessed thereof. Indeed, there is something to be said in excuse hereof, that is, the unsettledness of the country for a long time, the several changes of government it has undergone, and the small number of the English at present; and something to be objected, that is, that it would be first reasonable to settle religion among those who are professed Christians before we pretend to the conversion and settlement of the Indians. To which I answer, that, as what is passed must be excused, since it can't be helped, so, I see no reason in the objection, because a sufficient provision may be made, that one thing may be done and the other not left undone; especially when the Indians are so inclinable to receive the Christian faith, as they have made appear they are, both by that considerable number of the Mohawks whom Dr. Dellius has converted, (though by a method not so exact and prevalent as might be used,) and those Oneidas converted to Popery by the jesuit Millet, (see Note 25,) much to the advantage of the French, who have debauched so many of our Indians as they have made Christians, and obliged, by so doing, some of our Mohawks so much, that one of them, as I have heard, having run away from us to them, and, thereupon, being upbraided with his infidelity in forsaking his old friends, in his own defence made answer, that he had lived long among the English, but they had never all that while had so much love for him as to instruct him in the concerns of his soul, and shew him the way to salvation, which the French had done upon their first acquaintance with him; and, therefore, he was obliged to love and be faithful to them, and engage as many of his nation as he could to go along with him and to partake of the same knowledge and instructions that were afforded and imparted to him, so that it appears to be a work not only of great charity but of almost absolute necessity to endeavor the conversion of the five nations and other Indians, lest they be wholly debauched by the French, and become, by God's just permission, for our neglect therein, of faithful and true friends, as they have been hitherto, most dangerous and cruel enemies.

CHAPTER VII.

OF CANADA.

Canada, (see Note 26,) although not in this province, but far distant from it, is yet a great enemy to the peace and happiness of it. First, as it is the reason why the most fruitful part thereof lies at present waste, forsaken by its former inhabitants, and hindered as to its future improvements. Second, as it is the reason why His Majesty and the remainder of this province are at great charges in maintaining Albany and the frontiers against the insults of the French and their Indians. Third, as they debauch our Indians from their fidelity, and instruct them in popery, both which at present are, and hereafter will be, much to the damage of this province: add hereunto that, by the damage they do to the other provinces [of] New England, and are at all times ready to do, they put the king of England and his subjects to a great deal more charge to defend themselves than the king of France, or the jesuits (if it be their country, as some say it is) are at to defend Canada against us, though we are in all over twenty times their number; besides, the governors of New York that have been from time to time have so often promised our Indians, to encourage them to continue the war, that they would send for ships from England to come and wholly subdue and conquer Canada, that they, seeing they do not come, and that Sir Francis Wheeler, when at Boston, attempted nothing, begin to be discontented, and to charge the governor with breach of promise, and are very wavering in their fidelity and friendship towards the English; so that it appears a matter highly requisite to be endeavoured to conquer and subdue Canada, and that before it grow stronger in fortifications than at present it is; and, indeed, it is a shame it should not be effected, when we so much exceed them in strength in those parts, and when, if it please God to prosper us therein, we shall not only be freed from the charges which at present every province is at, more or less, but Canada may be so settled that it may be a great addition of strength and wealth to the English in America, without being, in a little time, any charge, but rather a benefit to the crown, as by a method to be laid down for the subduing and re-settlement of it, shall, as I trust, in due time and place appear. And now I have finished the consideration of the province of New York, and of those things therein or relating thereto which, being of greater moment or consequence, are worthy of blame and correction; and shall now lay down the means and method which I conceive proper for the remedying thereof, and thereby of advantaging and improving the country, which I shall do in three chapters: the first treating of the more general means; the second containing a particular method for the conversion of the Indians; and the third proposing a way for the subduing and resettlement of Canada.

CHAPTER VIII.

OF THE MORE GENERAL MEANS FOR CORRECTING THE EVILS IN NEW YORK.

The great, most proper, and as I conceive effectual, means to remedy and prevent all the disorders I have already mentioned, and promote the settlement and improvement of religion and unity, both among the English subjects that are already Christians and the Indians supposed to be made so, is, that his Majesty will graciously please to send over a bishop to the province of New York, who, if duly qualified, impowered, and settled, may, with the assistance of a small force for the subduing of Canada, by God's grace and blessing be author of great happiness, not only to New York in particular, but to all the English plantations on that part of the continent of America in general. I doubt not but this proposal may, at first sight, seem very strange and unlikely to be effected; but if what follows be duly weighed and considered, I believe it will not appear wholly unreasonable.

It has heretofore been usual in England, when and where the dioceses have been so large that the bishop alone could not suffice for the government thereof, to adjoin to him one or more suffragan bishops, each of which were wont to execute such power, jurisdiction, and authority, and receive such profits as were limited in their commission by the bishop or diocesan whose suffragans they were. Such an one, I humbly conceive, might be very well sent over to the north-east part of America, to to be there and act as suffragan to my Lord of London. To do this, as I doubt not his Majesty's power, so I cannot think my Lord of London will be unwilling; and I am sure the great distance of the country, being 3000 miles from England, the largeness of the provinces considered altogether, and number of the people, with the other particulars already mentioned, do sufficiently require it. In hopes, therefore, that such a proposal as this will meet with good entertainment, or with a charitable and candid construction, at the least, among those who can best promote it, I shall proceed to mention some things which will much conduce to the bishop's better entertainment and success (see Note 27).

And, first, I shall speak of his personal qualifications; second of the place of his residence; third, of the powers to be committed to him; and, fourth, of the provision to be made for his maintenance.

1.—Among his personal qualifications I must, in the first place, reckon his age, his learning, and his piety, which, being particulars not fit for me to speak of, I shall pass them by, and leave them to the prudent judgment and determination of that pious prelate whose suffragan he is to be. But because I am something acquainted with the humours and inclinations of the inhabitants of that country, I shall make bold to add, that it is requisite he be a person of an obliging temper and conversation, who, having power to compel, will rather persuade and win to obedience by kind acts and generous usage; one whose deportment must vindicate his person and place from contempt, and yet must be, when occasions require, so meek, complaisant, and free, that even the meanest may not have reason to count him proud. One whose generous soul must always aim at good and laudable actions, and whose humility and love to virtue must be so great and real as that he will not think much to submit to low condescensions, inferior means, and continual pains to bring a pious and possible design to perfection: one that can so justly esteem of riches as to think it a necessary care to manage his income well, that he may have wherewithal to forward and encourage a good work, and yet so little affect and love them, as freely to part with them to pious and charitable uses; and, lastly, one that will both constantly practice those eminent notes of true Christianity, love and charity, himself, and promote them among all those who call themselves disciples of the crucified Jesus.

2.—The place of his residence, as I have already

intimated, will most properly be in the province and city of New York, for which there are several reasons:—first, the healthfulness of the country, the air being clear and pure, and the climate most agreeable to an English constitution, so that few or none contract diseases on that account, but many are freed from them; second, because a maintenance will be more easily settled for him in this province than in any other, after the manner I shall presently set down; third, because this is the most proper place to begin a reformation of disorders in, which are here greater than any where else, and yet will be more easily regulated; and to settle the government of the church of England, a matter whose foundation being already laid, though at present hindered, will yet, with a little pains, be put into a good forwardness; fourth, for the site of it, this country is as much as may be in the midst of all the other English plantations, so that a bishop being placed therein, his good influences and care will be readily dispensed for the benefit of every part; fifth, because there are already such forces in this province, that is, 300 soldiers in his majesty's pay, as will be sufficient to awe troublesome and pragmatical spirits, if there be any so bold as to endeavour to make any disturbance upon his going over.

3.—The power and authority requisite for him are these following:—first, that he be consecrated bishop by the archbishop, and duly impowered by my Lord of London, so that he may act as suffragan bishop to him, not only in New York, but also in all the English provinces in that part of America; second, that his Majesty, uniting the provinces of New York, Connecticut, New Jersey, and Rhode Island into one government, will please (see Note 28,) to send him over governor thereof, allowing him all the powers and privileges granted usually to the governors of New York, with power also to go out of his province so often as he shall think good to visit the other provinces as bishop only, and to constitute, not only for the time of his absence but if he see necessary at all other times, a lieutenant governor under him.

Note, that this union of the four governments proposed is not of absolute necessity, only of great convenience, so that it may be omitted (especially if Canada be subdued,) and the bishop be made governor of New York only, with the powers and priviliges before mentioned.

4.—That a maintenance may not be wanting suitable to his place and the great ends he is to promote, neither for the present nor future, it is requisite,

First, that if his Majesty is pleased to unite the four governments into one, that then he will please also to allow the bishop, as governor thereof, £1500 per annum, out of which a reasonable part or portion shall be paid to the lieutenant governor; or if New York be continued as it is at present, and he sent over as governor thereof only, that then his Majesty will please to allow him £1000 per ann. salary (out of which the lieutenant governor to have a reasonable part,) and all the other profits, benefits, and privileges which the present governor of New York enjoys; and also leave and power to search for (if he please) and open royal mines, as of silver, etc., if he can find any such, either in Connecticut, Rhode Island, New York, or New Jersey, on condition that in so doing he make use of the service of negroes only, and to pay to his Majesty such a proportion of the metal as, the charges and goodness of the ore considered, shall seem reasonable.

Second, That, to make up the abatement of his salary by that part allowed the lieutenant governor, his Majesty will please, so soon as opportunity presents, to give him some considerable preferment in England that does not require his personal residence.

Third, That his Majesty will please to allow him all licenses of marriage and probates of wills, and other things usually belonging to the bishops of England, and at present withheld from my Lord of London, and these to be given to himself as bishop, and those who shall be sent after him to serve in that station, now only in the province of New York and its dependencies, but hereafter in the other provinces also, so soon as religion shall come to be fully established therein: these particulars, if granted, will well suffice for a present maintenance; but then we must not neglect to propose a method of providing and settling a future maintenance that may be peculiar to himself as bishop, when he is so only, not constituted governor, as at present he is supposed to be, but when some other gentleman is sent over in that station, that he may then have wherewithal to maintain his family and keep up hospitality. Besides what [is] already considered, that will then remain to him, these further particulars are necessary to be put in practice:—

1. That his Majesty will please to give him the farm in New York, commonly called the king's farm, for a seat for himself and successors, which, though at present a very ordinary thing, yet will it admit of considerable improvement; and since this farm, renting at present for sixty bushels of wheat per annum, in the whole at four shillings per bushel, amounting to £12 New York money, is at present an advantage to the governor, that I may not seem not to care how much I impoverish the governor so I enrich the bishop, I further propose that the bishop be obliged, when himself is not governor, to render an equivalent to the present rent, either by giving yearly so many loads of hay, or by settling so much land where he please, within two miles of New York, as shall be sufficient for that purpose, or to pay the sum of money itself, which shall be best approved of.

2. That his Majesty will please, by letters patent,

to grant him the propriety of the Mohawks land, that is, so much thereof as is now unpurchased of the Indians, on condition that the first improvement he makes thereof shall be to settle in one or two towns, as shall seem best, 100 English families, on 5000 or 6000 acres of good land, the whole to be settled on himself as bishop, and his successors; and, for his encouragement, so to do with all the other land to be improved by him afterwards, as shall be best for the particular benefit and advantage of himself and heirs.

And that the Bishop may be the better furnished for some particular works of charity, such as converting the Indians, building churches, settling houses and a maintenance for ministers, etc., it is further humbly proposed—

1. That his Majesty, the Bishops, and other charitably disposed gentlemen, will please to make some contributions towards building a church in New York.

2. That his Majesty and my Lord of London, will please to give him the best authority and directions that may be for the obtaining a part of the revenue settled in New England for converting the Indians, such as shall be thought convenient.

3. That his Majesty will please to allow a chaplain to the soldiers at Albany in particular (to be paid out of the advance of their pay) who are lately gone over, and to be sometimes changed with him at New York.

4. Lastly, it is necessary that the Bishop carry over with him five or six sober young ministers, with bibles and prayer books, and other things convenient for churches, as shall be thought best.

Whosoever goes over with these powers, qualifications, and supplies, shall in a short time (through God's assistance) be able to make a great progress in the settlement of religion, and the correction of vice and debauchery in those countries; and, to be a little more particular,—

1. To those several vices of irreligion, drunkenness, cursing and swearing, fornication and adultery, thieving, and other evils accompanying them, he may put a stop by causing the good laws of England already made to be put in execution, and by providing others where those seem or are deficient; and also,

2. Which will remedy likewise the second head of inconveniences, want of a ministry, by settling ministers in those towns already provided for by Act of Assembly in some measure, and, as he best can, by supplying them with what is wanting, both for their private necessities and for the public exercise of religion, as allotting to them or purchasing for them glebe lands, promoting the building of churches, ministers' houses, settling schools with salaries, &c., by endeavoring so soon as may be, to provide for other places which are not provided for by that act, by exhorting, and, where good advice and persuasions will not prevail, by compelling,

ministers to live piously and soberly, and give a good example to their flocks.

3. By not suffering any justice of peace to marry in the province within ten miles of the place where any minister dwells, and endeavoring to promote the establishment of the like law in other provinces where it may conveniently be done, by causing the ministers and churchwardens to keep registers of all christenings, buryings, and marriages, according as in England is by law appointed, and always to take great care to prevent the marrying of any persons who are either one or both of them already engaged or married to others.

4. And where this is duly taken care of, another inconveniency will be well provided for. Men, although at present of many and different opinions, yet may be reconciled, in a great measure, by a pious and prudent ministry, who will seek to reduce them by good exhortations, to oblige them by neighbourly and charitable kindnesses, to encourage them by their own practice to live in the fear of God, and in brotherly love and unity one with another.

5. And though this method will greatly help towards the removal of the fourth inconveniency, yet it will not be completed without the assistance of his civil authority; that is, by causing a proclamation, or, if it seem necessary, an Act of Assembly, to be made, prohibiting all people to reproach any person for having been of Leysler's

or the contrary party; to vex or sue one another in law for any evils suffered in those times, or since; or to do any thing that may tend to the widening the breach or continuing the remembrance thereof, commanding them to forget things past, and to forgive one another; to live in peace, and to associate together as they did before that division, and as if such a thing had never happened: and by shewing himself indifferent to both parties, encouraging equally those of them who show themselves honest and virtuous, and truly well affected to his Majesty's interest. Thus may these several inconveniencies already mentioned be well redressed; but as for the conversion of the Indians, and the conquest of Canada, they will require, each of them, a particular chapter.

CHAPTER IX.

OF CONVERTING THE INDIANS.

When I speak of converting the Indians, by Indians I mean, principally, those five nations which lie between Albany and Canada, and are called: 1, Mohawks or Maquaes; 2, Oneides; 3, Chingas; 4, Onundages; and 5, Penecas: (see Note 29,) of whom tho' most of the Mohawks are converted to Christianity by Dr. Dellius, and some of the Oneides by the jesuit Millet; yet the first not being yet established in any good order at all, and the last being converted to popery, I look upon the work as yet wholly to be done; and if what has been already done is not a disadvantage to it, yet that little advantage is gained thereby, except a demonstration of inclination of the Indians to embrace the Christian religion. And though I mention only the five nations, yet do I not speak of them so as excluding all other septs and nations of them; no—for I hope this, once performed and brought to a good pass, may be as a ground work to the conversion of all the rest, as opportunity shall present; yea, possibly may be improved so far as to render this part of the continent truly civilized, speaking the English language, and submitting to his Majesty's government. And to begin,—

First.—That the person who undertakes this work should be a person of great authority, ability, and power, that he may the better persuade with them, and be the more respected, and abler to go through with such a matter, are things of so great advantage, that if they were not things already provided for, do deserve certainly to be put in the first place; but it being proposed that the bishop himself who shall be sent over be the main-spring and mover in this work, I therefore, without saying more thereof, add,

Second.—That when he goes out of England he carry over with him one Dutch and English dictionary, interleaved with white paper; paper of several sorts and in considerable quantity, for writing and printing books thereon; nails, iron, glass, and lead, for the churches and ministers' houses; tools for joiners, carpenters, masons and glaziers, in such quantities as shall be thought convenient, or at least as the monies given for that purpose will allow.

Third.—That after his arrival there, he, with two other ministers whom he shall best approve of to be his assistants, set to learning that Indian language which is best understood by all the five nations; and for that purpose send for, and entertain in some employment about him, Mr. Arnhout, of Albany, (see Note 30,) the chief interpreter between the English and the Indians, who will be a great help to him in composing a dictionary, and learning the language; and get an Indian Bible and grammar from Boston, which will be likewise of some advantage to him

Fourth.—That after he can speak Indian well, and translate elegantly, he then, as opportunity shall best present, call all the five nations together, and endeavour, in a discourse composed for that purpose, to instruct them, and, by the best arguments he can, to persuade them to embrace the Christian faith and be baptized; in which if it please God he succeeds, as there is great hopes he may, then—

1st.—To desire of the five nations so many sober young men of each nation as he shall think convenient to live with him some time, and learn to read and write in their own language, and also to speak the English tongue, and read and write in the same; and some others, in number about twelve, to learn the trades of joinery, carpentry, masonry, and glazing; and, in the meantime, while they are learning these things, one of the two ministers shall be appointed to instruct the Indians in Christianity, as may best be done, and to bring over those who do not consent upon the first proposal.

2d.—While the other minister is learning the young Indians to read, etc. himself, with his assistance, may translate, as of the greatest use and necessity, the Common Prayer Book, the thirty-nine Articles, the Whole Duty of Man, and Patrick's Psalms; and then afterwards, as they best may, (   ) Short explanation of the Church Catechism, Dr. Hammond's Catechism, some short preparatory form for receiving the holy communion, a morning and evening Prayer for private persons, and a Primer for children, with a short morning and evening Prayer, and Graces before and after meat; so many copies of each to be printed as shall be thought convenient, and no other book besides them to be translated or printed in the Indian language, especially not the Bible, that the (see Note 31,) Indians, through a desire to read them, may be stirred up to learn the English language, and so at length may be induced to exchange that for their own; for otherwise, the Indian nations being so many, it will be almost an impossible work to convert them and provide for their civilizing and instruction.

3d.—After the young men can read and write well, and are acquainted with our language, customs, and religious service, the manner and way thereof (in which they, as also those put to trades, are to be inured as much as may be), and admitted to holy orders, then to dispose of them, settling one in every castle, except where two small castles are near to one another, for both which one may well suffice; and, for their better settlement, to cause to be built a church, a minister's house, and large room adjoining to it for a school, of wood or stone, as shall seem best and cheapest, (in which work the labour of those who learn trades will be very helpful); and after those things are perfected, gathering all the heads of the five nations together, to cause a maintenance by land to be settled for their ministry, that is the tenth part of their profit or income by hunting, fishing, fowling, etc., and of their corn and other fruits of the earth, with some peculiar advantages upon the account of their being schoolmasters, as it is intended they shall be. Those who are instructed in trades are to live among their countrymen, to teach them their arts; and that they may find employment, they are to be put upon building houses after the English manner, keeping cattle and fowls, ploughing the ground, and imitating the English in their other trades, ways of living, and customs, and one thing after another, that so, by degrees they may leave off their savage ways and become civilized, which, except it can be effected, it will signify but little to plant religion among them; therefore, so many other young sober Indians as shall be thought convenient may be taken in the places of those who are settled as ministers, and taught and instructed after the same manner they were, and put in their places too so soon as fit for it, either when any of them prove debauched, or improve not in knowledge, or neglect their duty (who in that case shall again be under instruction for their amendment or better information), or where any of them prove of eminent parts above the rest, and more sober and religious, who shall then be encouraged and allowed fit helps and instructions for the promoting the conversion of their neighbouring nations, which they may well do with the assistance of an English minister or two and the countenance of the bishop; and so in a few years, if this method be duly prosecuted, all the Indians on this part of the continent may, as 'tis to be hoped, be converted to Christianity; and, when they are civilized, may easily be induced to submit to the English government by the bishop, whom they must needs look upon, respect, and obey as their spiritual father, and one who will, to be sure, advise them as shall be most for their real benefit and welfare. And when they come to such a pass as that way can be made and means settled for arts and sciences to flourish among them, there is no doubt but many of them will become men of sufficient learning so that they may be instructed in the way of preaching, and have the full government and service of the Church of England settled among them, or acquainted with our laws, so as to be made magistrates, and govern the people by our statutes instead of their own rude and barbarous customs. The first of which when perfected, as it will be a great credit to the Church of England, so will the other be of great advantage to the civil state thereof; and both, I hope, tend to the glory of God and the eternal felicity of immortal souls.

But, till these designs can be fully accomplished, we must be contented to insist upon a method of religion that, though not complete as it should be, is yet such as the beginnings of Christianity among them will bear, and as is proper for weak teachers and ignorant hearers, and that to be this that follows:—

The ministers' duty in general among them is to be this: to pray for them, to read and administer the sacraments to them, to teach their children to read and to write, and speak English and their catechism, and to be thus ordered:

1st. He is to read Common Prayer among them (the lessons out of the Bible excepted) every Sunday and holyday, both morning and evening.

2d. On Easter Sunday, Whitsunday, the third Sunday in September, and on Christmas-day, after Common Prayer read in the morning and a psalm sung, he shall read to the people the thirty-nine articles of religion, and every other Sunday one portion of "The Whole Duty of Man," as they shall fall in order, and, when the whole is read out, shall begin again.

3d. Every first Sunday of the month, and on Good Friday, Easter-day, Whitsunday, and Christmas day, he shall administer the holy sacrament; and then the Sunday preceding such administration, upon notice thereof given, shall be read the exhortation in the Common Prayer-book appointed for that purpose.

4th. Every Sunday in the afternoon, at evening prayer, when the first and second lessons should be read in place thereof, after a psalm set he shall publicly catechise the children; those that are able to read, unto eight years of age, in the Church Catechism, from eight to twelve years of age in (   ) Short explanation thereof, and those from twelve to sixteen years of age in Dr. Hammond's Catechism, after which they may be admitted to the sacrament. The several catechisms shall be learned by heart by the children at home and at school.

5th. On the working days he shall teach the chidren to write, and to read, and to speak English; for their reading using a Horn-book, The Primer, the Church Catechism, etc.; for teaching English, to use those and the English translations of them, together with the other books, and also a grammar, with familiar dialogues to be composed for that purpose, and the Dictionary.

And by the just and constant observance of this method, there is no doubt but, through God's grace, they may be brought to and continued in a reasonable knowledge and practice of the Christian religion, till such time as, being thoroughly civilized, the whole discipline and government of the Church of England may be settled among them, and also duly practiced and observed by them.

CHAPTER X.

OF THE METHOD HOW TO SUBDUE AND RESETTLE CANADA.

I AM now in the last place to speak of the conquest of Canada, that is, how it may be effected, a business in which, though the Bishop is not so much concerned as in the former, especially as to the warlike part, yet may he be more than a cipher, yea, of particular consideration in the settlement of it, if it please God to permit it to be subdued, as in the sequel will appear.

What the strength and condition of Canada is at present is pretty well made evident by the account thereof which I sent over about ten or twelve months ago to the Right Reverend Bishop of London, a copy whereof I also had, which I lost (when I was taken prisoner) with my other papers, and in respect to that it is that this present method is laid down; and though it may be supposed, since that time, to be made rather stronger than become weaker, yet will it not, I think, be able to resist, if courageously invaded and prudently assaulted with the forces, and in the manner hereafter mentioned:—

1st. The first thing then to be done, in order to the conquest of Canada, is to pitch upon a general for the conducting and carrying it on; the general, then, is to be but one to command all forces, both by sea and land, that are sent or appointed for this purpose: for long experience has taught us, that equal and divided commands have ruined many noble undertakings and great armies. The wise and warlike Romans found this true, and, therefore, in their wars of greatest moment and danger, they generally had recourse to a dictator; and the success in the late invasion of Martinico has taught us the truth of it, wherein, as I have been credibly informed by impartial and eye-witnesses, the difference between the land and sea generals was the main, if not only, occasion of the miscarriage. As to his prudence, fidelity, experience, conduct, and courage, all great virtues and necessary in a commander, I have no need to speak thereof; his sacred Majesty, who is to pitch upon and commissionate him, being a most excellent and incomparable judge in those matters.

2d. The second thing to be provided for is forts, and warlike provisions sufficient for such a design, and these to be either sent for [from] England or prepared in America. The forces to be sent from England are proposed to be three ships of war of from forty to sixty guns, well rigged and manned according to their rates, furnished with all warlike provisions necessary for sea-service and maintenance of the men; as to which there may be six months provision of beer and water, and of beef, pork, oatmeal, peas, and bread, etc., for twelve months, canvass for 4000 or 5000 hammocks, or rather so many hammocks ready made for the forces that are to be raised in America; and, for the land service, 500 soldiers, well armed and accoutred, young, stout, well exercised, and, so far as may be, unmarried; twenty pieces of ordnance proper for battering of walls, with spunges, ladles, worms, powder, and bullets, etc., and two or three mortar pieces with granado shells, bombs, carcasses, spades, mattocks, and also powder and ball for the forces to be raised in America, that nothing may be wanting, though the enterprise prove much more difficult than is expected, it being much better to bring back ammunition than to fail in a design for want of it: however, as to the quantities and kinds thereof, I submit to better judgments, and shall only say that it will be a commendable care to see that the officers, both by sea and land, be such as are truly faithful and loyal to his Majesty. These ships, with all the particulars aforesaid, are to be ready to set sail by the middle, or, at farthest, by the latter end of February next.

The forces to be prepared in America, are to be these and in this proportion following:—New England 2000 men, Connecticut 700, Rhode Island and Martins-vineyard 200, New York 300, New Jersey 300, Pennsylvania 300, Maryland 400, Virginia 1000, and Carolina 300, amounting in all to the number of 5500, each man to have in readiness so much powder and ball as shall be judged requisite; and, if it be thought expedient, twenty carriages also may be made in New York for the twenty guns, to be sent over according to measures and directions to be sent likewise for that purpose.

The manner of ordering these forces and materials to be prepared shall be laid down under the next head, which is concerning the secrecy and privacy wherewith these affairs are to be carried on, which ought to be great so that the enemies may not get any foreknowledge of it; for, next to strengthening ourselves, nothing is more necessary than to endeavour to surprise our enemy, which is done, first by rendering him secure; second, by coming upon him unawares; and, third, by drawing away what strength or provision he already hath, as far as may be, from the place or places against which our designs are chiefly laid, which I conceive may be done by ordering affairs in this manner following:—

1st. To prevent all knowledge, or even suspicion, of what is intended by the provisions made at home and sent over, the ships may be pretended as convoys to the Must fleet, and to the Virginia fleet; and as to the stores put aboard them, it must be done as privately as may be, though, of itself, it be a thing that will not much 'be suspected, because it has been usual to send over stores to the American plantations, neither will the soldiers be much taken notice of, they being but 500; besides, they may be put on board at Plymouth suddenly, and under pretence of better manning the ships; or, if there goes a squadron of men of war to guard the fleet out of the Channel, it may be pretended that it is to inure them to the sea service; and then they may be disposed of to several other ships, as if they were to come back again therewith after having seen the fleet out of danger; and at sea they may be put aboard the ships in which they are to go to New York: in short, many ways may be thought of for the concealing the intention of so small a preparation, and that particularly pitched upon which will seem most likely and proper for the time. But, then, besides the orders given to the captains of the ships publicly, and for that purpose, they must likewise have other sealed orders given them very privately, with command not to break them open till a certain time to be appointed, that is, when they come to separate from the fleet, or when the fleet itself comes to separate, or, if they chance to be separated by foul weather, then to break open those orders wherein it shall be appointed them what port to go to, that is, New York; what commander to obey, that is the same who is made general of the land forces; how long to stay, that is, either till the design is effected, or till the coming out of some fleet according as the governor of the province where they are shall judge best for his Majesty's service; or if there be a great necessity and the ships proper, they may be sent out to cruise for privateers, or they may be ordered to visit Newfoundland by the way. One thing seems here proper to be mentioned, that is, that when these orders are opened, and the soldiers come to have some knowledge where they are going, their pay may be paid them till such time as they came aboard, and further advantages promised them for their encouragement.

It will not be amiss, if two French ministers, that are in orders of the Church of England, be sent over with these ships, for, if it please God the design prosper, there will be occasion for them.

2. For the more private carrying on of the design as to the forces prepared in the West Indies, it is convenient not to let it be so much as known to any person there (except that his Majesty shall please to communicate it to any of the governors) what is the true cause of raising the forces ordered

to be raised, and that may be done thus: It is now, while I am writing this, certain, that the French have a design upon the merchants trading on the coast of Guinea, and those trading into the West Indies. In order to the carrying on of the first, they are fitting out at St. Maloes four privateers, of from forty to fifty guns, and Monsieur de Gatine, commissary there, sent for one Captain —— Piles, and Henry Pinson his mate, both taken on board a small Guineaman, and having good knowledge of the coast and trade, and present condition of affairs there, to examine them concerning the same. And in order to the carrying on of the last, the English prisoners that came about four days ago, that is, October the 6th, last past, from Nants, do assure us, that the French are there fitting out seventeen privateers of from twenty-five and thirty to forty guns, whereof twelve are already rigged and fitted, to be manned in part with English, Scotch, and Irish, and to be sent to the West Indies, to interrupt and spoil our trade, and make prize of our merchantmen there. Hereupon occasion may be very well taken, and letters ordered to be written and sent with duplicates thereof by ships in December next ensuing, or the beginning of January, to every one of his Majesty's governors, and also to those of the proprietors, wherein to be signified to each of them, that there is certain intelligence from France of their fitting out divers ships of war, twenty or more, and that they are intended against our plantations in America. That, therefore, it is his Majesty's strict charge and command, that every one of them cause to be armed, in their several provinces, such a number of their choicest men as shall, by one, two, or three hundred, exceed the number before set down, and to meet at their chief port town by the 1st of April, and there to see that they be well armed, and every man provided with a proportion of powder and ball, to be appointed and to exercise them daily till further order; and, in the meantime, to see that whatsoever of his Majesty's ships are in their several ports, be cleaned and fitted for sea, so as to be ready to sail with the first order; and also to fit and prepare a sufficient number of good ships and sloops, and provisions of bread, beef, beer, pork, and peas, etc. for six months, in case there be occasion to transport the soldiers from their province to any other where it shall appear the enemy does chiefly intend his invasion, of which warning may be promised them by an express so soon as there shall be certain notice thereof.

And over and above this, orders may be sent to the Governor of New York, in particular, to make the twenty carriages as before; and to cause to attend at New York, from the 1st of April till further order, Robert Sanders of Albany, and five others that can give the latest and truest account of the present state and condition of Canada, without letting them know what they are caused to wait for, but only, in general, that it is for his Majesty's service; and that they shall be paid for the loss of their time, or else they may be kept under arms as men of special service and courage, which shall seem best to him, for concealing the true reason of their attendance. As for the carriages, he may pretend for the making thereof, that he has notice of so many guns of such a sort or bigness coming over, and order to have carriages for them in as much readiness as may be; that so soon as he has them they may be presently fitted for use, and planted where he shall think most convenient.

There may likewise with these, other orders be sent him, not to be broken open till the 1st of April, wherein it may be signified unto him that his Majesty, looking upon the French preparations as intended against New York, would send some ships of war over to his assistance, but that he immediately endeavour to stop any intelligence thereof from going to Canada. That he also send the several orders therein enclosed to the governors of the several provinces, to cause them forthwith to send away the exact number of forces chosen out of those armed and exercised according to former order, to the port of New York, he in the meanwhile to make all the preparation he can of victuals and lodging to entertain them, and, when they shall be arrived, to see they be well armed, and to exercise them, and acquaint them with the way of camping and engaging, till such time as the ships, and a commander-in-chief with them, shall come.

Again, to divert the enemy from the care of those places against which this design is chiefly laid, that is Quebeck, and their other places of greatest strength, a third order must yet be sent to the Governor of New York, appointing him to raise the Indians of the five nations, and to join with them 200 of the garrison and forces about Albany, 200 from New England, and 100 from Connecticut (for the obtaining whereof orders are also to be sent him by the first ships), and to have them ready, so that on the 1st of May they may be ready to march towards Canada; and there, by endeavouring, or pretending to endeavour, something that shall tend notably to the advantage of our party and the disadvantage of the French, as the fortifying and settling Cadaraque, or, seizing on some French garrison, to draw down the Governor of Canada and his forces towards them, but to take great care to keep in places of security, and not to be too active, but only while away the time, and delude the enemy, unless he sees he can gain a considerable advantage without any great hazard of his men.

Lastly, the commander-in-chief sent from England is to receive his commission for this service privately from his Majesty, wherein to be appointed commander-in-chief of all the aforesaid forces by sea and land, as well as those on Albany side as those which are to be transported by sea to Canada, with orders to sail directly for New York; and there, embarking his forces, with all possible speed, to make the best of his way for Canada, to prevent as much as he can any notice the enemy may have of his coming, and with instructions to make use of the foresaid Sanders and the others, appointed to give him information of the country and places of landing and advantages; to keep his soldiers from plundering, deflouring women, drunkenness, swearing, cursing, and all other debauchery; to proceed prudently, courageously, and valiantly, in the endeavouring to conquer Canada, till such time as it is thoroughly subdued, and then to return as shall be ordered and directed by his Majesty. There are other things to be added to his instructions in case he succeeds, which you will find couched among what follows.

In case, then, that this design succeed, his Majesty may please to appoint the bishop proposed to be sent over governor of New York, to be also governor of Canada, and every part and place thereof, as it shall come to be subdued, with power to constitute a lieutenant-governor thereof at his discretion, till such time as his Majesty's pleasure is further known; with power also, to appoint and order all matters ecclesiastical, and civil, as shall be best for the setting that province in the possession of the English.

Orders and instructions to be given, both to the

bishop as governor, and to the commander-in-chief, may [be] these:—

1.—That special and constant care be taken that the soldiers and seamen straggle not from the camp, nor plunder the country, burn houses, or destroy the corn, either growing or in the barn, nor the cattle of what sort soever, but that they preserve all things as in a country which it is hoped may come through God's assistance to be their own; and, therefore,

2.—All provisions, of what sort or nature soever, whether for man or beast, are to be secured for and given notice of to the governor and commander-in-chief, or either of them, that they may appoint what quantities thereof shall be sufficient for the maintenance of the army, or the prisoners, or victualling the ships for their voyage homeward.

3.—All prisoners are to belong to the King (slaves only excepted), to be civilly treated and used, and to be disposed of as the governor shall appoint, which may be after this or the like manner:—those who are of best quality, with the priests and other religious persons, to be sent home to England by the ships of war; two hundred families of husbandmen that are willing to stay, to be left and settled upon reasonable and encouragable terms, as tenants to those gentlemen and others to whom lands shall be given; three hundred or four hundred families more to be appointed for New York, where, if they are willing, they may be encouraged by the bishop to settle on vacant land, and in time may be converted to Protestantism by French ministers sent over for that purpose, and obliged to learn and use the English tongue and religion, and all the rest may be divided proportionably to each province, to be carried thither in the ships belonging thereto, where they may be encouraged to settle if they will, and, if it be thought for the weal of the province to encourage them, or otherwise to be sent prisoners to England in merchant ships, as opportunity shall present.

4.—All the ships taken in the voyage thither, or in port there, to be condemned in the first English port they come to, and to be disposed of by the governor there, as is appointed by law in such cases. And all towns, forts, castles, houses, instruments of husbandry, as ploughs, carts, harrows, etc., and working cattle, as horses, oxen, asses—and all warlike provisions, as great guns, small arms, powder, ball, swords, bagonets, etc., and the whole country, improved, or unimproved, to belong to the king, and to be disposed of by the governor as shall be best for his majesty's interest and advantage, and encouraging their settlement of the province, except as in the article following.

5.—All things belonging to religion and ecclesiastics, as churches, monasteries, nunneries, with the grounds and estates belonging to them, as also the money, plate, books, and all things in them and belonging to them, as horses, cows, sheep, instruments of husbandry, household stuff, and also the books found any where in other houses, to be given to pious uses, and to be disposed of by the bishop, and settled as shall seem to him best for the encouragement of religion in Canada, New York, or elsewhere, in any other of the English provinces; only to be excepted, that if there be any goods or chattels, whether money, plate, household stuff, or other things proved not to belong unto religious persons or uses, but put there only for concealment and security, etc., they are, in that case, to be delivered up, and ordered by the bishop to be laid to the common spoil, and, as such, to be divided with the rest among the soldiers.

6.— All other goods, not before excepted, whether money, plate, slaves, household stuff, or merchandize, etc., shall be gathered together and divided between the officers and soldiers, as is usual to be done in such cases; in which division the governor shall have an equal share with the commander-in-chief, and the rest according to their proportion. And, for the better and more equal division, it shall be appointed, 1st, That all men concerned in the service, seamen or soldiers, shall have part of the spoil without being defrauded or cozened thereof. 2d, that the Indian goods, as duffels, shirts, knives, hatchets, etc., be particularly set apart to be given to our Indians as their part of the prey, and, if there be any overplus thereof, it shall be given to those who shall remain in the country to trade therewith, either with our own Indians or those of Canada, who, if they will submit quietly, shall not be suffered to be prisoners to our Indians, but reckoned friends to us, as at present they are to the French. 3d, That every man, of what rank or quality soever, shall be bound to deliver up to the common heap all the spoil he shall get of what nature soever; and that whatsoever they shall find in houses or any other place which they cannot bring away, they shall not spoil it, but leave it undamaged for the benefit of those who shall afterwards come to settle there; and that whosoever shall offend in either of these particulars shall, by so doing, forfeit his part of the spoil, and be otherwise punished as the commander-in-chief shall think fit.

7.—All the arms and warlike stores taken from the French to be carefully gathered together, and laid up in the fort of Quebeck, and other convenient places, and there kept in good order and condition, so as to be at all times ready for use. All places of strength and great advantage, and disabled in the taking, or any ways in need to be better fortified, shall be duly taken care of and fortified in the best manner that may be, and furnished with great guns and stores convenient for the defence thereof; for which purpose the guns and mortar-pieces carried over, together with any taken by the way, or in harbour there, or on land, with sufficient quantities of powder, ball, etc., shall be left there, to be disposed of in each garrison as shall seem necessary.

For the resettlement of this province the governor may—

1.—Appoint a house and land and other conveniences for the bishop, and houses, lands, etc. for the ministers out of those belonging before to and set apart for that use, with schools, a library, etc. as best may be done.

2—Dispose of the lands, houses, instruments of husbandry, etc. on such terms and with such provisions as shall be reasonable and proper for the King's profit, the landlord's advantage, the tenant's encouragement, and the clergy's maintenance; and that, first, to those of the soldiery from England, who, being married, will settle there and send for their wives over; and, second, to those who being unmarried, and of those soldiers or of the forces come from any of the neighboring provinces, and desirous to settle and marry there any of the French maids or widows (such as they can prevail with), to every man according to his quality, place, and merit, and as shall seem best to the governor.

3.—Send to England, desiring encouragement may be given to the French Protestants to come over and settle there with their families, which it is believed many of them will willingly do, if they be assured to have lands, houses, etc., given to them on reasonable terms, as it is intended they shall. And this is the method which I promised to lay down as proper for the subduing and resettlement of Canada; which, if it be not so complete as it ought to be, or not likely to be so effectual as I hoped it might, in the judgment of understanding persons, if yet it will serve but as the first lines of a draught, or a motive only to enable heads to do better, I shall not only be contented, but very glad, and not think that I have lost my labour.

SOLI DEO GLORIA.

MR. MILLER'S INFORMATION

Furnished to the Commissioners for Trade and Plantations, Sept. 4, 1696.

"That there are about 3000 Families in New York and about 5000 Families in Connecticut

That he was at Albany when the French came down that way in the year 1693. It was into the Mohacs Country, beyond Schenectidy. There were of them about 2 or 300, and as many of their Indians. The Force sent against them was from Albany much about the same number (English and Indians) under Major Schuyler, who speaks the Indian Language. Other forces sent from New York came too late. Major Schuyler's Order from Colonell Ingoldsby who commanded in Albany was that when he found he was near the Enemy he should fortify himself; He did so; And in the mean time while sent out detachments who in several attacks killed about 30 or 40 of the French party, whereupon the rest fled and have not since returned. This was the only incursion of any moment that was ever made upon that Country before his coming away in June 1695.

That the town of Albany is fortifyed only with stockado. There is but one Minister of the Church of England and one Schoolmaster in the whole Colony of New York. A Dutch minister there had instructed some Indian children. But the English in New York had not endeavoured it. There are many interpreters.

That the Trade of Albany is chiefly Beaver. Formerly it may have been to the value of £10,000 a year but is now decay'd, by reason of Warr between our Indians and the French, not diverted to any other place. The burdens also of that Province have made 2 or 300 families forsake it, and remove to Pensilvania and Maryland cheifly and some to New England.

That the presents usually given to the Five Nations are not distributed to particular Men amongst them: But in general to the whole. It is done in the Governor's name as by order from the King. Their returns are in Beaver and Otterskins to the value of 20 or 40 £. Those presents of theirs are made to the Governor: He is doubtfull if not sometimes mentioned for the King.—*New York Col. Documents,* iv, 182.

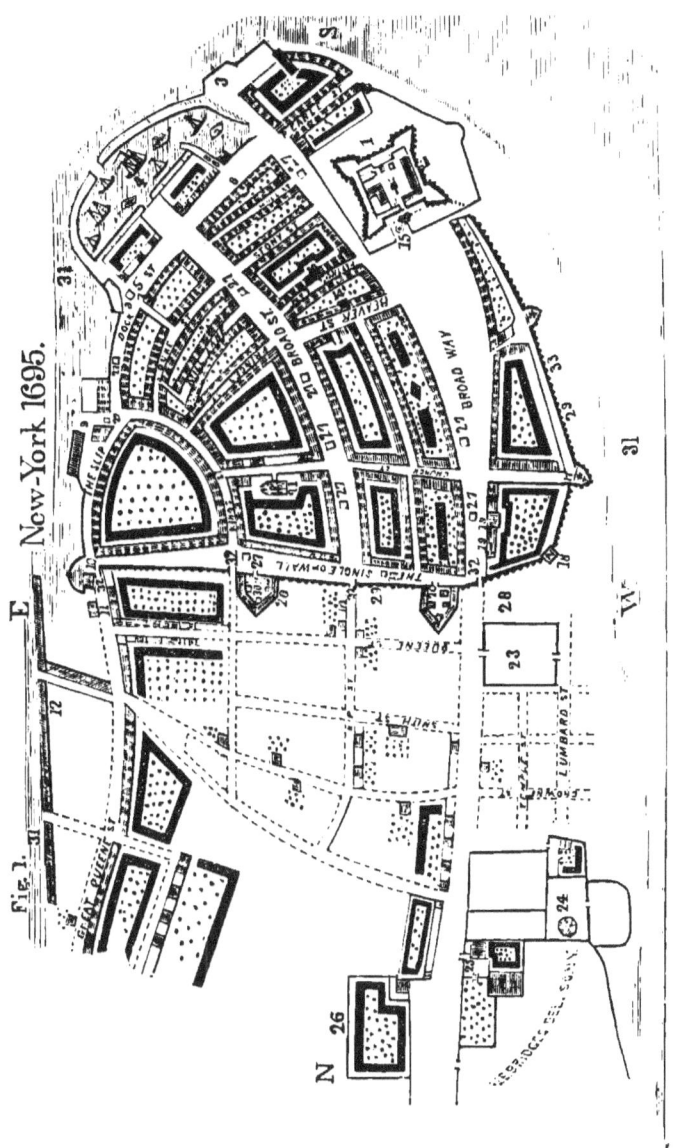

THE EXPLANATION OF FIG. 1.

1. The chappel in the fort of New York.
2. Leysler's half moon.
3. Whitehall battery of 15 guns.
4. The old dock.
5. The cage and stocks.
6. Stadthouse battery of 5 guns.
7. The stadt (or state) house.
8. The custom house.
8. 8. The bridge.
9. Burghers, or the slip battery of 10 guns.
10. The fly blockhouse and half moon.
11. The slaughter-houses.
12. The new docks.
13. The French Church.
14. The Jews synagogue.
15. The fort well and pump.
16. Ellet's Alley.
17. The works on the west side of the city.
18. The north-west blockhouse.
19. 19. The Lutheran church and minister's house.
20. 20. The stone points on the north side of the city.
21. The Dutch Calvinist church, built 1692.
22. The Dutch Calvinist minister's house.
23. The burying ground.
24. A windmill.
25. The king's farm.
26. Coll. Dungan's garden.
27. 27. Wells.
28. The plat of ground designed for the E. minister's house.
29. 29. The stockado, with a bank of earth on the inside.
30. The ground proper for the building an E. church.
31. 31. Shewing the sea flowing about N. York.
32. 32. The city gates.
33. A postern gate.

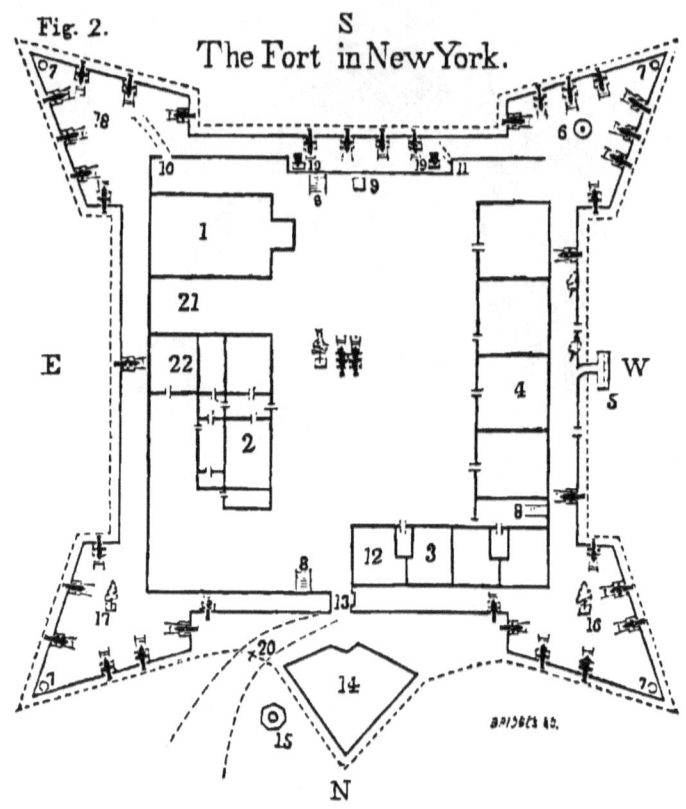

THE EXPLANATION OF FIG. 2.

1. The chappell.
2. The governor's house.
3. The officers' lodgings.
4. The soldiers' lodgings.
5. The necessary house.
6. The flag-staff and mount.
7, 7. The centry boxes.
8, 8. Ladders to mount the walls.
9. The well in the fort.
10. The magazine.
11. The sallyport.
12. The secretary's office.
13. The fort gate.
14. A horn-work before it.
15. The fort well and pump.
16. Stone mount.
17. The Iron mount.
18. The Town mount.
19, 19. Two mortar pieces.
20. A turn-stile.
21. Ground for additional building to the governor's house.
22. The armory over the governor's kitchen.

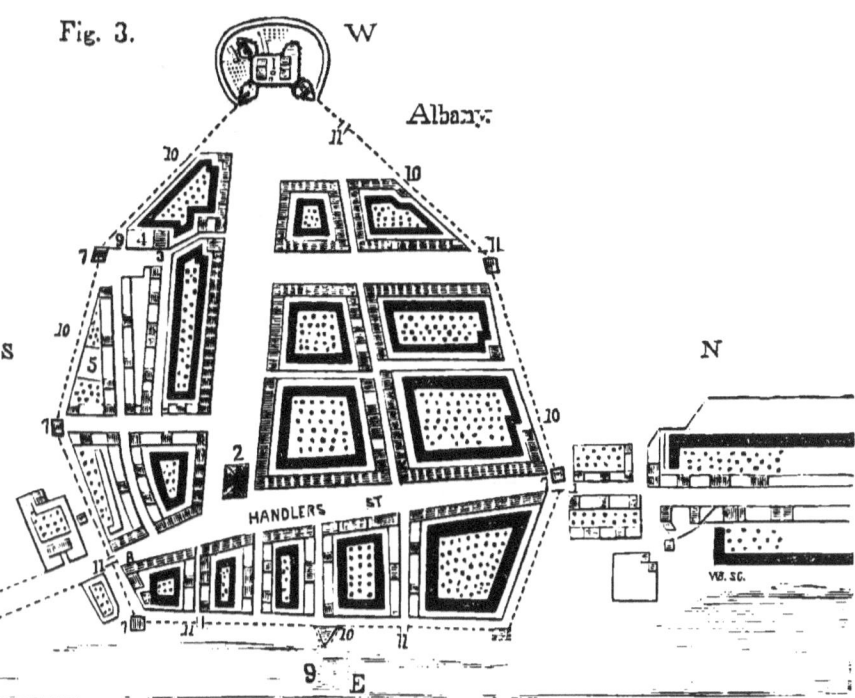

THE EXPLANATION OF FIG. 3.

1. The fort of Albany.
2. The Dutch Calvinist church.
3. The Dutch Lutheran church.
4. The burying place.
5. The Dutch Calvinist burying place.
7, 7 The block houses.
8. The stadt-house.
9. A great gun to clear a gulley.
10, 10. The stockado.
11, 11. The gates of the city, six in all.

THE EXPLANATION OF FIG. 4.

1. The governor of Albany's house.
2. The officer's lodgings.
3. The soldier's lodgings.
4. The flag-staff and mount.
5. The magazine.
6. The Dial mount.
7. The Town mount.
8. The well.
9. 9. The centry boxes.
11. The Sally port.
12. 12. The ditch fortified with stakes
13. 13. The gardens.
14. The stockado.
15. The fort gate.

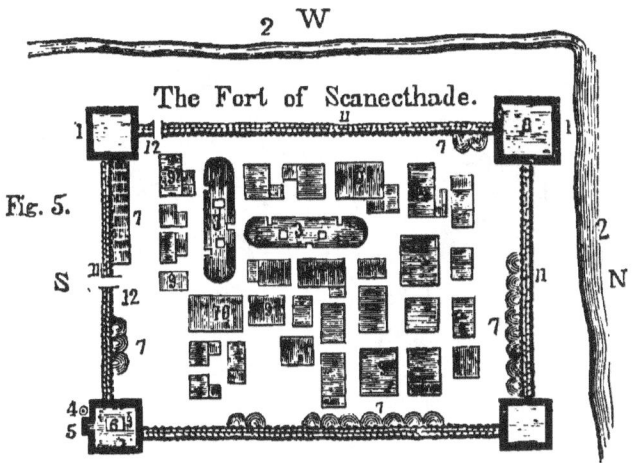

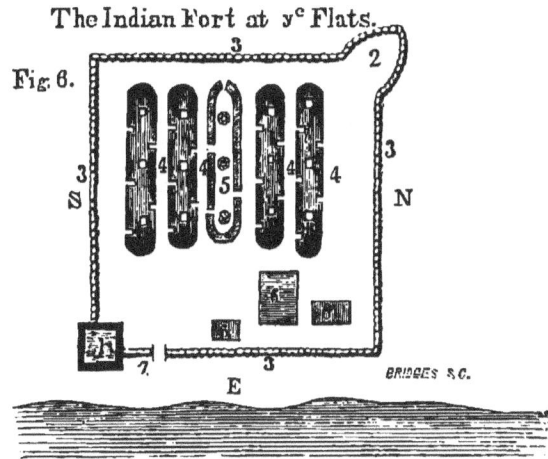

THE EXPLANATION OF FIG. 5.

1. 1. The blockhouses.
2. 2. Rivers running beside the fort.
3. 3. Indian wigwams.
4. The flag-staff.
5. A centry box.
6. The spy-loft.
7. 7. The sties for hogs.
8. The blockhouse, designed for a church.
9. 9. Those and others like them are houses.
10. A great barn.
11. 11. The treble stockado.
12. 12. The fort gates.

THE EXPLANATION OF FIG. 6.

1. The blockhouse.
2. The mount.
3. 3. The stockado.
4. The Indian houses or wigwams covered.
5. A wigwam open.
6. Houses for the soldier's use.
7. The fort gate.

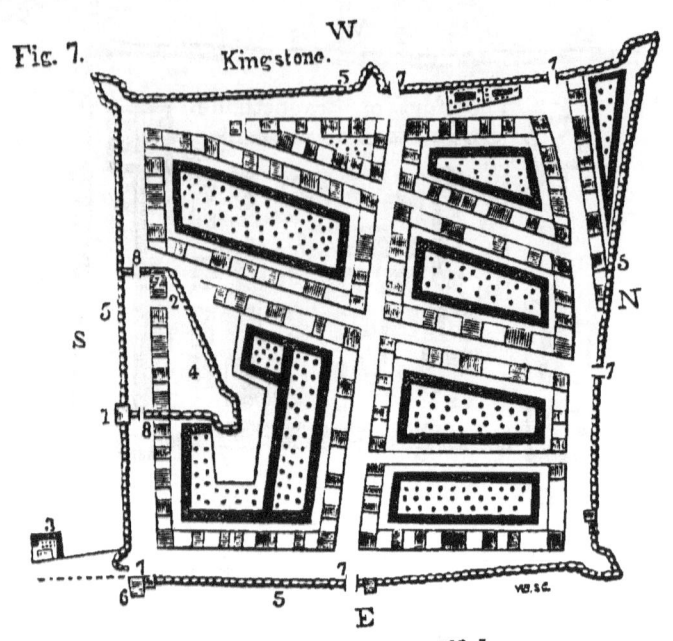

THE EXPLANATION OF FIG. 7.

1. The blockhouse.
2. 2. The church and burying place.
3. The minister's house.
4. The part separated and fortified.
5. The Stockade.
6. The house where the governor is entertained.
7. 7. The town gates.
8. 8. The gates to the separate fortified part.

NOTES.

Note 1, *page* 26.

HENRY COMPTON, Bishop of London, to whom Miller addresses his work, was the youngest son of Spencer, Earl of Northampton, and born in 1632. After his education at Oxford, he remained abroad till the Restoration, when he became a cornet in a regiment of horse. Disliking the army, however, he entered the church. He was made Canon of Christ Church, Oxford, in 1669, became Bishop of Oxford in 1674, and the next year of London, which see he filled till his death in 1713. He had superintended the religious education of the princesses Mary and Anne, daughters of James, and was a strong upholder of the Church of England, against Dissenter and Catholic. During the reign of James, he was for a time, in fact, suspended, and his powers vested in a commission, so that we naturally find him among those who welcomed William. He crowned that prince, and for a time enjoyed his favor, but lost it, as did all of the high church party. During Anne's reign, he regained part of his former influence. As a prelate, he seems to have been zealous and disinterested, giving large sums to rebuild churches, and increase the income of poor vicars. In the affairs of America, he was one of the first of the English bishops who took any considerable interest. He was the author of *A Treatise on the Holy Communion*, 8vo., 1677; *Episcopalia, or Letters to his Clergy*, London, 1686; *Letters to a Clergyman*, 1688; *A Charge*, 1696; *Ninth Conference with his Clergy*, 1701; *Letter concerning Allegiance*, 1710; besides being translator of one or two minor works, but he attained no eminence as a man of letters. By the Charter of Gov. Fletcher, he was made the first Rector of Trinity Church, New York.

Note 2, *page* 28.

The name of Long Island was changed to Nassau Island in 1692.—*Laws of the Colony of New York* (ed. 1719), page 17. But the name never obtained, and it still retains its original and appropriate title. On De Laet's map appears the name Matouwacs. Early French maps call it the Isle of the Holy Apostles and Ascension Island. An English colony on a grand scale was projected here by Ployden, and a very curious tract written at the time, exalting the advantages of the island, has been recently printed, entitled: *The Commodities of the iland, called Manati ore Long Ile which is in the continent of Virginia.* Staten Island means Island of the States, and was so called in honor of the States General of Holland.

Note 3, page 28.

The Counties received their names under James, and nearly all refer to him and the Stuart family. Kings and Queens were named after Charles II, and his Queen Mary; Duke's County, now in Massachusetts, and Dutchess were named after James and his wife; New York, Albany and Ulster, represent his titles on the English, Scotch and Irish peerages, and Orange was named in compliment to the Prince of Orange, who deprived him of his crown.

Note 4, page 28.

The length in a straight line is only 13 miles from the Battery to Kingsbridge.

Note 5, page 29.

The Stadthouse or Town Hall, was originally at the head of Coenties Slip, and was erected in 1642, by Kieft as a tavern, but in 1652, on the organizing of the city government, became the Stadt Huys. This house was the scene of some important events. Here, in 1664, the articles of capitulation were signed, which became the law of the colony, here too, the surrender of the colony to the Dutch again was made. It was made the first school house in 1652, and the first Court of Admiralty was held here in 1668. In 1696, a plan was adopted for a new city hall, at the head of Broad street, where the custom house now stands. This was completed in 1700, at a cost of near £4000, and the old Stadt Huys was sold for £920. This new city hall was that in which Washington was inaugurated president.

The fortifications at the Stadt Huys in 1688, were "a half moon most ruined and washed away by the sea," with three demi culverins.

Note 6, page 29.

The Burgers Path was the present Old Slip. This too, in 1688, was stated to be "most ruined and beaten down by the water." Its armament was four seekers and one *minion*. The reader who wishes to compare the state of the fortifications further will find a full description of their condition in 1688, in *Valentine's Manual* for 1855, p. 551-3.

Note 7, page 29.

Scanectade (Schenectady), is the Mohawk. The name means beyond the openings. It was given by the tribe to Albany, and retained on the division by the present town.

Note 8, page 29.

NESTIGAYUNA. According to Dr. O'Callaghan (*N. Y. Colonial Documents*, IV, 184), "Canesteguine is laid down on Mitchell's Map of North America, 1755, and on Sauthier's Map of the Province of New York, 1779, on the north bank of the Mohawk river, a little west of the Cohoes Falls, in what is now Sarataga county." Lord Cornbury (*Ib.* IV, 968), says that it was fourteen miles from Albany in the woods. The Half Moon was fourteen miles above Albany upon the river (*Ib.*). Colonel Römer, the engineer, in 1698 (*Ib.* IV, 440, 682), represented the forts at Albany and Schenectady as wretched, and like Gov. Fletcher and his successors, urged the erection of regular stone forts there, and the restoration of the forts at Kanestigionne and Half Moon, as the barriers of the frontiers.

Note 9, page 34.

WINE. The culture of grapes for manufacture into wine, early attracted the attention of Europeans, especially of the Spaniards and French, who were practically familiar with the proper mode of cultivation and the process of wine making. Full half a century before a plan was formed for colonizing Long Island chiefly to raise wine. Even in Canada, the missionaries inaugurated it by making wine of wild grapes for altar purposes, as early as the middle of the seventeenth century, and a good table wine was, it is said, made at Montreal not long after; but the French government, with the jealousy usual at the time, prohibited the planting of vineyards and the enterprise was accordingly abandoned. Some French colonists in Rhode Island, also manufactured wine about this time.—*N. Y. Col. Doc.*, IV, 787. Massachusetts sought to establish vineyards at an early day, and Governor's Island was granted to Winthrop in 1632, on condition of his planting a vineyard there.—*Young's Pilgrims*, 152.

In more recent times vine growing has been carried on with great success. The failure of imported vines induced the attempt to improve the native grape, and these have succeeded beyond all expectation. The Catawba grape and wine have acquired more popularity, and have given wealth and name to Nicholas Longworth of Cincinnati. In New York, the largest vineyards *are those of Dr. Underhill at Croton Point.*

In 1769, the government of Virginia embarked in vine growing, under the direction of Andrew Estave, but the experiment failed, and the lands and negroes were sold in 1776.—*Hist. Mag.*, IV, 219.

Note 10, page 34.

From the enumeration of roots it would seem that the potato was not yet cultivated to any extent, and it probably was not for thirty or forty years after. Potatoes are mentioned as being purchased for the dinner on the inauguration of President Leverett at Harvard College in 1707.—*Hist. Mag.*, V, 184.

Note 11, page 34.

The Dutch name for Shad was *Elft*, which also meant *Eleven*. Misled by this, or in jest, the early settlers called the Streaked Bass, Twaalf (*i. e.* Twelve), and the Drum, Dertien (*i. e.* Thirteen).—*Benson.* This gave rise to the statement here made by Miller.

Note 12, page 35.

MANUFACTURES. New York early attempted manufactures, and at this time, traded largely in staves, cloth stuffs and hats; but this spirit of enterprise did not harmonize with English views. Lord Cornbury well expressed those views in these words: "All these Colloneys which are but twigs belonging to the Main Tree (England), ought to be kept entirely dependent upon and subservient to England, and that can never be, if they are suffered to goe on in the notions they have, that as they are Englishmen, soe they may set up the same manufactures here as people may do in England, for the consequence will be that if once they can see they can cloathe themselves, not only comfortably but handsomely too, without the help of England, they who are already not very fond of submitting to Government would soon think of putting in Execution designs they had long harbourd in their breasts."—*Cornbury to Sec. Hodges.* Cosby, at a latter date, wrote to the Board of Trade in regard to the prejudicial increase of hat making (*Letter of Dec.* 18, 1732), and Smith (vol. II, p. 278) notes that "hats were exported to the West Indies with great success, till lately prohibited by an act of Parliament."

Note 13, page 37.

REV. HENRY SELYNS was ordained at Amsterdam, Feb. 16, 1660, for the Church at Breuckelen (Brooklyn). He officiated there and at the Governor's Bowery from September, 1660, to 1664, when he returned to Holland. Declining an invitation in 1672, he returned to this country in 1682, on the death of Mr. Drisius, and was pastor of the Reformed Dutch Church in the city of New York, until his death in 1701, being the eighth in succession from Dom. Michaelius. He was a man of learning and a poet, and his reputation was not confined to the Dutch nation and its colonies. He seems too, to have been laborious in the ministry. In the Leisler troubles, he, like most worthy men, incurred the hostility of the self-created governor.—*O'Callaghan's Col. Doc.*, III, 646. As a poet, he is in point of time, next to Steendam, and Mr. Murphy states that a MS. volume of his poems exists.

Note 14, page 37.

REV. P. PEIRET signed the address against Leisler in 1690 (*Col. Doc.*, III, 748-9), and died in 1705.—*Doc. Hist. of New York*, II, 247; III, 250.

Note 15, page 37.

As to Saul Brown, Dr. Fischel kindly informs me that he was simply a merchant, who officiated for a short time as reader in the Synagogue. He came to this city from Newport, R. I., where he had a brother David, whose name appears in the petition to the Assembly of Rhode Island, in behalf of the Jews of Newport, June 24, 1684.—*Bartlett's Colonial Records of R. I.*, III, 160.

Note 16, page 37.

REV. DAVID DE BONREPOS was a French Protestant minister, who accompanied the first Huguenot emigrants from France. He was the first minister at New Rochelle, but the industrious historian of Westchester county can give us no details as to his labors, and we know the fact merely from a letter addressed by him to Leisler.—*N. Y. Doc. Hist.*, II, 304. In 1695, he was, as here stated by Miller, on Staten Island, but the next year describes himself in a deed as of New York.—*Bolton's Hist. of the Church in Westchester Co.*, 396.

Note 17, page 37.

It is an extremely curious fact, that the Mr. Vesey, dissenter, "without orders," here referred to by Mr. Miller, should almost immediately become the first resident Rector of Trinity Church, a benefice to which Mr. Miller himself had laid claim. The Rev. Wm. Vesey was a native of Massachusetts, and if we can believe Lord Bellomont, the son of a Jacobite, who had been pilloried at Boston for his adherence to the cause of the unfortunate James II. William was graduated at Harvard in 1691, and seems almost immediately to have gone to Long Island, where he was at the time Mr. Miller wrote.—

Doc. Hist. III, 265. When a body of church wardens and vestrymen was created for New York, they asked in 1695, the opinion of the Assembly as to their right to call a dissenting minister, and being sustained by that body called Mr. Vesey. Trinity Church was erected about the same time, and as Mr. Vesey was popular, Gov. Fletcher seems to have induced him to conform to the Church of England, and become Rector of Trinity. He accordingly proceeded to Boston, and was received into the Church of England, and armed with necessary documents, sailed for England, where he was ordained. He officiated for the first time as Rector of Trinity, on the 6th of February, 1697, and continued to discharge the duties of his post for nearly half a century, dying on the 11th of July, 1746.

Note 18, page 37.

Mr. Mot was probably the Rev. John Morse, minister of Newtown. Alarmed by the act of 1693, which they regarded as an attempt to enforce the establishment of the Church of England, and provoked at it, as imposing an unjust burthen on them, the people of Newtown, resolved that "the town will call a minister to preach the gospel amongst us upon liking." They accordingly invited Mr. John Morse, born at Dedham, Mass., March 31, 1674, and graduated at Harvard in 1692. He officiated at Newtown, from Sept. 15, 1694, till his death in October, 1700. His ordination seems to have taken place in 1697.—*Riker's Annals of Newtown*, 126-131.

Note 19, page 37.

"The young man coming to settle in Westchester without orders," was Warham Mather.—*Bolton's Westchester.*

Note 20, page 37.

The Rev. Godefridus Dellius, was Dutch minister at Albany, from 1682 to 1699, and during much of the time, a conspicuous character in the affairs of the colony. He came over in accordance with an agreement made by contract at Amsterdam, July 20, 1682, by which he was to officiate as assistant minister at Albany, for four years from his leaving Texel at 800 guilders per annum in beaver or 600 bushels of wheat.—*Munsell's Annals of Albany*, I, 105; VI, 80. He missed the vessel on which he was to sail from England, and had to return to Holland, but finally arrived in August, 1683, when a subscription was made to meet his salary.—*Ibid*, I, 105.

He did not seem to have formed much attachment to the New World, as in 1685, he accepted a call to Heuclem, and was about to return to Holland; but he evidently married and settled down, laboring not only among the

Dutch, but also among the Mohawks, of whom he was the first Protestant missionary, and over whom he acquired great influence.

Leisler found in Dominie Dellius, one not disposed to recognize his authority. A letter of Father Lamberville to the Dutch clergyman, thanking him for an act of kindness to Milet a missionary held captive at Oneida, was in Leisler's eyes, sufficient ground for putting Dellius in prison, in 1690.—*N. Y. Col. Doc.*, III, 732. On getting free he retired to New Jersey, Long Island and finally to Boston. Sloughter recalled him in 1691.—*Ibid*, 772. Under Fletcher, he enjoyed great influence, and was employed to treat with the Indians. He availed himself of the occasion to obtain a grant of an immense tract of land, afterwards set aside as extravagant and illegal. The Earl of Bellomont at first regarded him with favor, and sent him with Schuyler to Canada in 1698, but soon after complained of him in the most violent terms, and brought such accusations against him that he was deprived of his church and ministerial function by act of the legislature in 1699.—*Col. Doc.*, IV, 510.

On this he proceeded to England, and subsequently, it is said, to Holland.—*Annals of Albany*, I, 88.

His register shows many Indians baptized and received as church members, from 1689 to 1699 (*Ib.* I, 96-101, II, 163-174, III, 61-82), the first being an Indian, aged 40 years, of the Ockkweese, Arnout Viele being sponsor. It was proposed to send Dellius out in 1705, as a missionary of the Propagation of the Gospel, but Col. Heathcote opposed it.—*Doc. Hist.* III, 124.

He was alive in 1714, and applied to the Assembly for some arrears due him, part of which he obtained.—*Annals of Albany*, X, 223.

Dr. Dellius seems to have been a worthy clergyman, enjoying the esteem of his own flock, of the Catholic clergy of Canada, of the Episcopal clergyman at New York, of the New England divines, as well as of the Bishop of London and his own Church; and we must conclude Bellomont to have been prejudiced. The extent of Dellius' knowledge of the Mohawk, and his labors seems to have been, however, limited.

Note 21, page 40.

As Miller wrote while Fletcher was still in power, he makes no allusion to the piracies by which New York merchants of that day profited, yet the cases of Coats and Tew could not have been unknown to him, nor the part taken by the merchants in Hoare's cruises. As it was a time of war, Fletcher issued commissions to enable them to act as privateers against the French, but the real object was well known, and Fletcher's conduct led to his recall and to the appointment of Lord Bellomont with strict orders to stop all piracy. His attempt to do so by means of Capt. Kidd, and the piratical course of that commander are well known; but the end was effected, Kidd was the last of the New York pirates, and our merchants turned to less lucrative, but less criminal investments. An account of the whole subject will be found in Valentine's *Manual* for 1857, p. 455-479.

A communication evincing much research touching the history and fall of Capt. Kidd, was drawn up by the Hon. Henry C. Murphy and published in the *Democratic Review*, between 1840 and 1850.

Gabriel Furman, Esq., the editor of the new edition of Daniel Denton's *Description of New Netherlands*, 1670, was an enthusiastic believer in the authenticity of a report which obtained great currency about 1840, that nearly all the ill-gotten treasures of Capt. Kidd, which were supposed to be very large, lay at the bottom of the Hudson river, near Caldwells, a little below Peekskill on the opposite shore.

He had amassed a large amount of material obtained from every accessible source, respecting the life and exploits of this famous outlaw, which he had intended to be given to the public in due time, but alas, alas, that grim and inexorable messenger, death, put an untimely stop to his useful career, as has been the case with thousands upon thousands of others, and will continue to be so as long as frail man inhabits this wandering globe.

Note 22, page 43.

MR. MILLER is here greatly in error. The States General of Holland in 1590, directed marriage to be performed by a magistrate, and the law was in force in New Netherland till the conquest. By the Duke's *Laws*, published March 1, 1664, title *Marriages*, it was made lawful " for any Justice of Peace to joyne Parties in Marriage." See the title in *N. Y. Hist. Society's Collections, Series* 1, I, 362. This has never been altered and is to this day the law of the state of New York. The rule of the Catholic Church which prevailed prior to the Reformation, does not require the intervention of a clergyman to perfect the marriage, the parties themselves forming the contract, and the officer, civil or ecclesiastical, being merely the witness thereto, and this is the law in New York.

That bigamy prevailed we may infer from the fact that one of Mr. Miller's immediate successors, the Rev. Symon Smith, was presented by the grand jury in 1699, for marrying Elizabeth Buckmaster, wife of Edward Buckmaster, to Adam Baldridge.—*Hist. Mag.*, VIII, 189.

Note 23, page 46.

The only Episcopal clergymen up to this time in the colony, if we except the Rev. Nicholas Van Rensselaer (ordained by John Earle, Bishop of Salisbury, 1663-5), were the chaplains to his Majesty's forces. These were:

1678-80, Rev. Charles Wolley, A. M. 1683, Rev. Dr. Gordon. 1684-6, Rev. Josias Clarke. 1686-9, Rev. Alexander Innes. 1693-5, Rev. John Miljer. 1699-1700, Rev. Symon Smith. Rev. —— Brisac. 1704, Rev. Edmund Hott. 1704, Rev. John Sharpe.

The establishment of the Church of England, however, dates from the conquest. As the kings of England from the time of Henry VIII., united in their persons the papal and regal powers, the extent of ecclesiastical was conterminous with that of the regal, and where the sovereign was king he was head of the Church, and the Church consequently existed in the eye of the law.

By the articles of capitulation of the Dutch authorities, in 1664, it was agreed that: "The Dutch here shall enjoy the liberty of their consciences in divine worship and church discipline;" but the English then in the colony, or those who might thereafter come in, could not claim any such privilege, nor Dutch or English claim exemption from the payment of church rates as established in England.

New York from this time was deemed a part of the diocese of London, or a dependence on the metropolitan see of Canterbury. The Duke of York, however, as a Catholic, felt doubtless no especial zeal in establishing the Anglican Church, and if a chaplain of the Established Church attended his expedition, his name does not seem to have been recorded.

The Duke's *Laws*, promulgated in 1664, directed: 1. The erection of a church in each parish; 2. Eight overseers to be chosen by the householders of the parish, who with the constable were to choose two as church-wardens; 3. Ministers to produce to governor, proof of ordination by some Protestant bishop or minister in some part of his majesty's dominions or the dominions of some foreign prince of the reformed religion. The duties of overseers were, among other things, the making and proportioning the levies and assessments for building and repairing the churches, provision for the poor, and maintenance of the minister. Subsequent laws directed churches to be built in three years, reduced the number of overseers to four, and at last imposed a double rate in towns that had not made a sufficient maintenance for their minister.—*Duke's Laws, New York Hist. Soc. Coll.*, 1, I, 336, 407, 428.

In 1674, James, by an order of July 1, established a regiment at New York, with a chaplain, who was to receive a salary of £121 6s. 8d., "to commence from ye time ye Soldiers come on board and to be paid at New Yorke, and to be estimated after ye rates of Beaver there."—*N. Y. Coll. Doc.*, III, p. 220.

The first of these chaplains, the Rev. Charles Wolley, is the first clergyman of the Church of England of whose labors here we have any record. He was the author of a *Journal of a Residence in New York*, published in London, in 1701, and reprinted by Mr. Gowans of New York, in 1860. In the introduction to this latter edition, Dr. O'Callaghan has given the result of his labors to trace the history of the pioneer of the Episcopal Church in the city of New York.

The place of ministration was the chapel in Fort James, and even this was for many years shared with the Dutch clergyman and his congregation; but from 1674 a regular series of Episcopal chaplains succeeded, as to whom, however, we have few details.

In 1677, the Bishop of London, whose jurisdiction extended to all the colonies, complained of the neglect to establish a ministry in the various colonies (*Ib.*, page 253), and the next year Andros wrote: "The Duke maintains a chapline which is all the certaine allowance or Church of England, but people's free gift to ye ministers."—*Ib.*, page 262.

This condition lasted till James' accession to the throne, the Legislature convened in 1683, which established freedom of worship, making no change in the state of affairs. In 1686, Dongan wrote: "The Great Church which serves both the English & the Dutch, is within the Fort, which is found to bee very inconvenient therefore I desire that there may be an order for their building another, ground already being layd out for that purpose, & they wanting not money in Store wherewithall to build it."—*Ib.*, page 415.

King James found the machinery of the government in the hands of a party who controlled him and his successors, and the plan of actually establishing the Church took a decided form. The instructions sent out to Dongan in 1686 differ essentially from those which emanated from James, as Duke. This Catholic governor, under a Catholic king, of a province where the mass of the people were Dutch Calvinists, was required to see that the Book of Common Prayer was read every Sunday, and the Blessed Sacrament administered according to the Rites of the Church of England. No minister was to be preferred to any benefice without a certificate from the Archbishop of Canterbury, whose power in matters ecclesiastical was to extend to all but the collating to benefices, marriage licenses, and probate of wills, which important points were reserved to the governor.—*N. Y. Col. Doc.*, III, 688.

During the two ensuing years we find nothing done, however, to carry out this part, the governor being doubtless not over zealous in the matter.

Some most strangely have assumed Leisler's conduct to have been a struggle in behalf of the Dutch Church against the Established Church; but, unfortunately, the documents all militate against this convenient theory. All parties were so unanimous in their denunciations of James and Catholicity, that no domestic clashings of Protestants appear. Nicholson, who alone represented the Church of England, retired. The council who claimed to hold the reins of government, were mostly of the Dutch Church.—*Ib.*, p. 588. And on the other hand see *Leisler's Letters to the English Bishops.* Leisler, though a deacon in the Dutch Church, was no friend of the Dutch or French clergymen in the city.—*N. Y. Col. Doc.*, III, 646, n.; 651, n. Of an Episcopalian party at the time no trace appears in any document, and the only Episcopal clergyman, the Rev. Alexander Innes, who had been chaplain in the fort from 1686, took his departure soon after the commencement of the troubles, bearing, as Leisler states, testimonials from the French and Dutch clergymen. The Episcopalians must have been few ("Here bee not many of the Church of England" (*Ib.*, 616), said Dongan), or they would have organized as a Church, like the Dutch and French Calvinists and the Lutherans.

Leisler's acts were not recognized in England, where Nicholson had been regarded as lieutenant-governor, and Sloughter subsequently appointed. The latter was sent by the Dutch Stadtholder, as king of England, to rule over former subjects of Holland; but the power that controlled the Catholic James, controlled the Reformed Dutch William, and the latter, like the former, gave his governor of New York instructions to establish the Church of England. The instructions to Sloughter are a copy of those to Dongan, with the additional injunction as to the maintenance for each orthodox minister.—*N. Y. Col. Doc.*, III, 688.

Sloughter on his arrival made this an early object of his care. On the 18th of April, 1691, the Assembly, on the recommendation of the governor to introduce a "Bill for settling the Ministry and allotting a maintenance for them in each respective City and Town within this Province, that consists of Forty Families and upwards," sent to the attorney-general to draw such a bill. The act as framed, was read on the 1st of May, but, "not answering the intention of the house, was rejected, and ordered that another be brought in."—*Journals of the Assembly*. The explanation of this is, doubtless, that the attorney-general drew such an one as would lead to the establishment of the Church of England, in conformity with Sloughter's instructions. The death of the governor left the matter in this state, yet the subject was not entirely dropped. On August 23, 1692, it was ordered that a bill may be drawn for the better observance of the Lord's day, and that each respective town within this province have a minister or reader to read Divine service. But Col. Benjamin Fletcher, the new governor, was a man zealously attached to the Church of England. On his arrival and at the first meeting of the Assembly he urged the settlement of a ministry. The house took it up reluctantly. On the first of April, 1693, it was "Ordered that the Committee formerly appointed for the settling of the Ministry and Schoolmasters do forthwith proceed upon that business."—*Journal*, 30. But the session came to a close without any action in the matter, which drew out a sharp rebuke from the governor.—*Smith's New York*, I, 130. When the new Assembly met in September, he again recommended the matter in such urgent terms, that a committee was appointed on the 12th, and three days after, their report was read and approved, and "It was ordered that a bill be brought in for the establishment of it (a ministry) accordingly." The speaker on the 19th, brought in a "Bill for settling the Ministry and raising a maintenance for them in the City and County of New York, County of Richmond and Westchester, and Queen's

County." It passed two readings, and was referred back. On the 21st it came up again amended, and passed the house, who transmitted it to the governor. The next day Fletcher and his council returned it with an amendment, requiring the minister, when called by the wardens and vestry, to be presented to the governor for approval and collation, but the house replied, "that they could not agree thereunto, and pray that it may pass without that amendment, having in drawing of the bill due regard to the pious intent of settling a ministry for the benefit of the people."

The governor replied to the house warmly, declaring that he had by letters-patent right to collate or suspend any minister in the colony (*Ib.*), but nevertheless gave his assent to the bill.

The act of Sept. 22, 1693, obtained by so much endeavor, did not on its face establish the Church of England. It provided that a good sufficient Protestant minister to officiate and have care of souls should be called, inducted, and established within a year in the city and county of New York, one in Richmond, two in Westchester, and as many in Queens; 2, that New York and Westchester should each raise £100 for the maintenance of their respective ministers; 3, that ten vestrymen and two church-wardens should be annually chosen by all the freeholders; 4, that wardens pay the maintenance to the minister in four quarterly payments.—*Laws of the Colony of New York.*

We have seen that under it Fletcher claimed the right of inducting: the Rev. Mr. Miller, the writer of this tract, took a broad view of it. Considering apparently that the act established a benefice or living, and that the governor by his commission had the right of presentation, he, in February, 1694, demanded to be inducted into the parish of Trinity, but his claim was not acknowledged.—*O'Callaghan, Col. Doc.*, IV, 182, n.

The vestrymen and church-wardens were actually chosen, and seem even to have acted. In 1695, five of them, a minority, applied to the Legislature to know whether they could call a dissenting clergyman, and the Assembly gave it, as their opinion, that they could.—*Journal*, 53. April 12, 1695.

Meanwhile the Episcopalians in the city of New York began, under the encouragement of Fletcher, to take steps to organize, and build a church, and having secured the ground commenced the erection of Trinity. On the 6th of May, 1697, Caleb Heathcote and others, "present managers of the affairs of the Church of England in the City of New York," petitioned Fletcher for a charter. This petition recites the act of 1693, that there was then no Church, that petitioners had built one, asks to be incorporated, and that the maintenance given under the act be assigned to the pastor, and a grant of lands near the church be given.—*Doc. Hist.*, III. The governor on the same day issued a charter in the name of the king, though by what authority does not appear, which recites the act, assumes it to apply solely to the Church of England, incorporates the managers as church-wardens and vestrymen of Trinity

Church, declares it to be the only parish church, and then proceeds: "And our Royal pleasure is, and we by these presents do declare that the said Rector of the said Parish Church is a good sufficient Protestant minister, according to the true intent and meaning of the said Act of Assembly, made in the aforesaid fifth year of our Reigne, entitled an Act, &c.; and such we do further of our like speciall grace, certain knowledge and meer motion, give, grant, Ratify, endow, appropriate, and confirm unto the said Rector and his successors forever the aforesaid yearly maintenance of £100."

The rector named in this charter was the Bishop of London, whose income was thus increased by a tax levied on all the inhabitants of the city of New York, and this by a mere act of the governor against the intention and will of the Legislature. It would be curious to study the details of this transaction, and ascertain how Fletcher was able to carry it through, as he apparently did, without eliciting a protest from the members of the Reformed Dutch Church; but the submission was to all appearance absolute, and though some of Fletcher's extravagant grants were set aside, including a lease to Trinity Church, in August, 1697, no allusion is made to the charter of Trinity, and by the consent of the governed, the church-wardens and vestrymen to be elected by all the freeholders of the city, under the act of 1693, found most of their powers vested in the church-wardens and vestrymen of Trinity Church elected by the Episcopalians only.

Dr. Berrian in his *History of Trinity Church* (page 13), is singularly inaccurate as to this charter. He says: "In the fifth year of the reign of William and Mary, 1697, by an act of Assembly, approved and ratified by and with the consent and authority of the Governor, a royal grant and confirmation were made of a certain church and steeple, &c." But there is no such act in the Colony Laws, and 1697 was not 5 William and Mary, and Fletcher's Royal Charter, is the only known charter of Trinity.

Note 24, *page* 51.

It would not be easy to give a more guarded and temperate account of the Leisler rebellion, than that here given by Mr. Miller. Leisler's conduct became a party question, and the popular party made him their great martyr. Yet it is very evident that he was neither the champion of the rights of the people as against the aristocratic element in the colony, the champion of the colony as against the mother country, nor the defender of the Dutch church and its liberties, against the encroachments of the Church of England. All these grounds have been taken at different times, but the documents of the period show no tokens of such struggles as to call for any championship of the kind. Leisler seems to have been a vain, ignorant, ambitious man, deluded perhaps in the outset, by a belief in the plots his fancy conjured up, but once in a little power, resolved to push it to its utmost. Mortified at the treatment of the government in England which totally ignored him, he in a fit of disappointed ambition, resolved to resist the Governor actually sent out. He fired on the troops from England, and shedding blood, deserved his fate. Yet his execution was a political blunder; it became the stock of a party which for years, by its triumphs and defeats, retarded the prosperity of the colony. His Life by the talented Charles F. Hoffman, in Sparks' *American Biography*, is almost a romance, and we must await the day when O'Callaghan or Brodhead shall write the history of New York in that day, as now revealed, to have the real history of Jacob Leisler. For our own part, we add merely these few data:

Jacob Leisler was a German, who came out as a soldier in the West India Company's pay, in 1660. After the English conquest, he became a merchant, and acquired wealth. In a voyage to Europe, in 1678, he was taken by the Turks, and forced to pay a heavy ransom. In 1683 he was appointed Commissioner of a Court of Admiralty. In 1689, he usurped the government; In 1691, he was taken by Gov. Sloughter, tried, convicted, and May 16, 1691, executed.

The *Documentary History of New York*, II, 1-250, and the *Colonial Documents*, III, 572-796, contain the chief materials on Leisler's reign.

Note 25, page 53.

The Rev. Peter Milet was a Jesuit missionary who came to Canada prior to 1667. He went to Onondaga in 1668, on the invitation of and in company with the celebrated Garacontié. He labored here till 1671, when he replaced Bruyas at Oneida, and made this his missionary field till 1684, when on the breaking out of war, he proceeded to the camp of De la Barre. He was chaplain at Fort Frontenac in 1687, when Denonville seized the chiefs, and remained there till June, 1689, when, lured out to attend a dying Indian, he was taken prisoner and with much ill-treatment hurried off to Oneida. Here he was doomed to die, but he was too well known, and too much esteemed. His life was spared, a matron having adopted him. In this condition as a prisoner he remained till October, 1694, a source of great trouble to the colony of New York, the Indians refusing to give him up or send him home. After his return to Canada he remained on the mission till after 1701.

The anecdote of the Indian mentioned here by Miller is found elsewhere, the Indians frequently making the contrast as the Abnakis did in Maine, and the Iroquois in the next century in regard to Oswegatchie.

Note 26, page 54.

The French colonies in North America, now represented solely by the little islands of St. Pierre and Miquelon, include on a French map a hundred years old all north of Mexico, except Florida, and a very narrow strip along the Atlantic. Its history begins in the unrecorded voyages of the Basque and Breton fishermen, the voyages of Verrazani and Cartier. Its first settlements were Port Royal, founded in 1604, and Quebec, founded in 1608. These colonies, were, however, neglected by the French government, which seems to have regarded them only as a field for the operations of the fisher or fur-trader, or the nobler operations of the Christian missionary. When an English force under Argal destroyed Port Royal in 1612, France scarcely noticed it, and when another English expedition, led by a refugee named Kirk, reduced both Quebec and Port Royal in 1629, the French government made so little effort that she recovered possession only in 1632 of the ruins. From this point, however, the colonization proceeded more rapidly, checked only by a constant war with the Five Nations south of Lake Ontario, whose hostility was a necessary consequence of the friendship of the Hurons of Upper Canada, and the Algonquins of the St. Lawrence. The nearest Europeans to the Five Nations were the Dutch, who by supplying them with arms rendered them a deadly scourge to Canada. Had the French Government at all regarded the value of its colony, it would have purchased or wrested New Netherland from Holland, and thus have controlled the Iroquois. Even New England, whose friendly Indians were molested by the Mohawks, would have viewed the step without alarm. But France lay dormant, till one day the Governor of Canada marching to reduce the Mohawks, found the English flag waving at Albany, and learned that the English king had ordered his governor of New York to unite with Connecticut and Massachusetts in reducing Canada. The Dutch had, but from avarice, aided the Five Nations; with the English it was policy, and from this date, February 22, 1666, when Charles II first ordered it, for a hundred years New England, New York and the Five Nations were stimulated in every way to crush Canada. Religious fanaticism was evoked, and the extirpation of their Roman Catholic neighbors was made so completely a part of their religious feeling, if not religious creed, that it furnishes the key to most of the events of the succeeding century, and when baffled by the power which called it forth contributed in no small degree to hasten the American Revolution, and still influences politicy and literature. But while England thus menaced Canada, France was not idle. She now, too, began to plan the conquest of New York and of Boston; and from the date of the English Revolution of 1688, the Border war continued till the fall of Canada.

M. de Callières in 1689 proposed the conquest of New York, but the plan resulted only in the attack on Schenectady; the next year Phipps attacked Quebec by sea, hoping to be supported by Winthrop by way of Lake Champlain, but the latter was unable to proceed, and Phipps repulsed, enabled Louis XIV to commemorate by a medal the liberation of Quebec.

The French then repeatedly invaded the territory of the Five Nations, and in 1701 hoped under Iberville to reduce New York, but in 1709 New York and New England, under Colonel Vetch and Francis Nicholson, made another attempt to invade and conquer Canada, but the plan again failed, and the troops never took the field. In 1711, however, the attempt was again made by a land force under Nicholson, and a fleet under Sir Hovenden Walker, but Walker's fleet was wrecked on the St. Lawrence, and as before Nicholson's army dispersed.

In 1745 the French retaliated by advancing into New York and destroying Saratoga. This led to another abortive Canada expedition in 1745-6. Still pursuing the plan of subduing the French province, a triple army took the field in 1755; but Braddock was defeated and killed on the Monongahela by Beaujeu, and in New York the troops did not, even with their defeat of Dieskau, make much progress towards conquest. In 1759, Amherst again led an army northward, but winter set in before he could enter Canada. Wolfe's victory at Quebec, however, opened the way, and in 1760, Amherst's army of English and provincials entered Canada in triumph, and the wishes of the colonies nurtured for three quarters of a century were gratified.

The toleration which England granted the Canadians was quite naturally in the eyes of the colonists a grievous wrong. It contributed in no small degree to hasten the revolt of the older colony, and in 1775 an army entered Canada to wrest it from England, whom they had aided to capture it. Foiled then, America in 1812 again endeavored to accomplish her long cherished design, but having again failed, the flag she helped to rear above the homes of the French still waves.

Note 27, page 57.

The first proposal for an American Episcopate, of which we have any authentic record, was in 1672 or the year following. In one of these years, a resolution was taken by the king (Charles II) in council, to send a bishop to Virginia, and the individual was actually selected on whom the proposed honor should be conferred. Dr. Alexander Murray, who had been the companion of the king in his travels, was the person nominated to be the first bishop in America.—*Dr. Hawks. P. E. Hist. Society Coll.*, I, 137.

Note 28, page 60.

This union of the Colonies was a subject frequently brought up. It was one of James II's ideas, and William attempted it. The endeavor to unite Connecticut to New York is well known, and the appointment of Bellomont to Boston and New York was a reverting to the days of Andros. In the *New York Colonial Documents*, there is a curious summary of the reasons of the different colonies for opposing such a union. William Penn's plan of such a union will be found in vol. IV, p. 296.

Note 29, page 66.

The Iroquois consisted of five nations, Mohawks, Oneidas, Cayugas, Onondagas, Senecas, occupying the heart of what is now the State of New York. The Mohawks lay on their river of that name, the Oneidas, Onondagas, Cayugas, successively to the west, near their lakes, and west of all, towards the Niagara, lay the Senecas. These names, except the first, are corruptions of their own. The Mohawks called themselves Gagnieguehague, but as the tribe collectively was styled Ganniagrari, the She Bear; the neighboring Algonquin tribes called them Maqua, the Bear, a name which the Dutch and English accepted.

These five nations formed a league, and in their idea, constituted a complete cabin, hence the name for the whole was Hotinonsionni, meaning "they form a cabin."

The family of tribes to which they belonged was widely extended. On both sides of the Niagara were the Attiwandawonk, or Neuters, absorbed by the Senecas, beyond them, on Lake Huron, were the Tionontates, or Dinondadies, now called Wyandots, and dwelling in our west; still further on, were the five nations of the real Wyandots, of whom one nation and fragments of others were absorbed by the Senecas, and other Iroquois tribes, and such as escaped war and famine removed to Quebec.

Some distance inland, to the south of Lake Erie, lay the Erie; east of them the Tiogas; on the Susquehanna the Andastogues, or Susquehannas, called Minquas, by the Dutch. The Patuxents and Piscatoways, of Maryland, were apparently of the same stock, and so certainly were the Meherrin, Nottoway and Chowans, of Virginia. The Tuscaroras of Carolina, were the most southerly tribe of the family * unless we are to class the Cherokees as really belonging to it.

---

* Mr Gallatin supposed this family divided into two groups, but he failed to identify the Susquehannas with the Andastes, and had confounded these last with the Guyandottes, who were simply the Wyandots, both words being English forms of the name which the French wrote Wendat. The Iroquois origin of some of the Maryland tribes he had not observed, and we may hereafter identify some more of those in Virginia as belonging to this family. We possess vocabularies of the following dialects. 1 Hochelaga, 2 Wendat, 3 Tionontate, 4 Mohawk, 5 Oneida, 6 Cayuga, 7 Onondaga, 8 Seneca, 9 Susquehanna, 10 Nottoway, 11 Tuscarora.

The five nations, or Iroquois, according to their own traditions and those of the neighboring tribes, dwelt formerly on the St. Lawrence, as far down as Gaspé, Quebec, and Three Rivers. The Algonquins drove them back, and Cartier, in 1534, found their first village on the Island of Montreal, although some were still intermingled with the Micmacs.

Of their history during the rest of the sixteenth century, we are almost entirely ignorant. The Mohawks, in a war with the Susquehannas or Andastes, had been nearly annihilated. At the beginning of the seventeenth, we hear of the Iroquois through the French in Canada, the Dutch in New York, the English in Virginia. Champlain having secured the friendship of the various Algonquin tribes on the St. Lawrence, and of their allies, the Hurons in Upper Canada, hoped by active hostilities to drive the Iroquois to peace; and in May, 1609, set out with a war party of Hurons and Algonquins to attack the Mohawks. They ascended the Sorel to Lake Champlain, and on the 29th of July, met and defeated a Mohawk war party, on the banks of the Lake. The next year the French and their allies, defeated another party on the Sorel, and for some years the Mohawks, deterred by fire-arms, seem to have held aloof.

Meanwhile Champlain had proceeded to the Huron country, and in September, 1615, joined an expedition against the Entouhonorons, apparently the Onondagas, and in October attacked their fort, but failed to take it, although Champlain built a tower to overtop their palisade. This victory elated the Iroquois Cantons, who had secured the friendship of the Dutch by the treaty of Tawassgunshee, in 1618. Obtaining fire-arms, they invaded Canada in 1621, attacked a French party near Montreal, and invested Quebec. A short lived-peace was concluded in 1624. Full of proud defiance, they continued the war with the Mohegans, and in 1625 killed the Dutch commander at Albany, Van Krieckebeck, who had rashly joined a Mohegan war party.

This victory made the Dutch henceforth neutral, and the fall of the French power in Canada gave the Iroquois time to deal such blows on the Hurons and Algonquins that they never recovered. In vain did the French, who recovered Canada in 1632, endeavor to shield their allies. The Iroquois war parties scoured the country far and near, spreading on all sides the terror of their name. Whether from policy or from accident, they rarely cut off English settlers.

In 1639 they destroyed Ehwae, a town of the Dinondadies; in 1642, cut off the Hurons from the French, and defeated the Huron flotilla under Ahasistari. The missionary Jogues then taken and led to the Mohawk. Though a party of Mohawks was repulsed at the walls of Fort Richelieu, the next year they led another missionary in triumph to their village. They also destroyed another Huron town, and cut off many parties of Algonquins, notwithstanding the skill and bravery of the able Pieskaret.

In the summer of 1645, the Mohawks made peace with the French and their allies, at Three Rivers, and the French hoped by converting them to Christianity to make the peace durable, but Father Jogues, the missionary, on proceding to their town, in 1646, was put to death. They plundered Three Rivers in 1647, cut off by treachery their great antagonist, Pieskaret, and completely ravaged the Huron territory.

The force sent out by the League must have been very large. Every strategic point near the French settlements or on their trading routes was occupied, and a large army entering the territory of the Hurons and of the Attiwandaronks, or Neuters. The Hurons lost many, and deeming their frontier too exposed, abandoned Taenhatentaron and St. Johns.

But the Iroquois, on the 4th of July, 1648, took and destroyed the fortified town of Teananstayae, or St. Joseph's, killing the missionary Daniel and his flock.

After destroying the town of St. Ignatius, in March, 1649, they attacked the strong town of St. Louis, which after severe loss, they carried by storm, putting all to death, the missionaries Brebeuf and Lalemant expiring in the most exquisite tortures. An attempt was then made on the town of St. Mary's, but the Hurons made a stand before the town, and though defeated, the Iroquois suffered too severely to think of advancing.

The Huron nation was destroyed; one tribe, the Scanonaerat and a part of the Arendahronon, submitted to the victors, and removed to the Seneca country. Fifteen towns were burnt by the inhabitants, who fled in various directions, some to the Tionontates, some to the Eries, others to the Andastes on the Susquehanna. The missionaries with one remnant remained at St. Mary's, but in the spring removed to Charity Island in Lake Huron, and the whole Huron country was deserted.

The successful Iroquois the next year surprised one of the Dinondadie towns and the remnant of that nation dispersed, a part joining the fugitive Hurons on Charity Island. The Neuters were completely subdued in this campaign, and absorbed by the victorious Iroquois, who carried them off, leaving the whole of Upper Canada a desert.

In the following year they pursued the remnant of the Hurons and Dinondadies, who abandoned Charity Island, the former chiefly descending to Quebec, the latter retreating to Manitouline, where after surprising an Iroquois party, they were for a time unmolested.

In 1651, the Mohawks nearly annihilated the Attikamegues or Whitefish Indians above Three Rivers, and blockaded that French town, killing the governor, Duplessis Bochart, who attempted to raise the siege. In an attempt to take the town, however, the Mohawks lost their great war chief, Aontarisati, but they kept up the seige and menaced Montreal and Quebec; but at last proposed peace.

At the same time Onondagas came to Montreal, as the Eries were waging a harrassing war on the western cantons. Peace was accordingly made in May

1653. In pursuance of this peace a part of the Hurons on Isle Orleans removed to Onondaga, and the Jesuit missionaries began their labors in the Iroquois cantons. The menacing attitude of the Eries and Susquehannas induced them to invite a French colony, and Dupuis, in 1655, began a settlement at Onondaga which proved but of short duration. The Iroquois invaded the Erie territory with a large force led by Achiongeras, and after an obstinate fight took Gentaienton, a considerable town, slaughtering an immense number. A few subsequent campaigns caused the Erie name to disappear. The Onnoutiogas, Ahondi, Atiragenratka, Gentaguega, Atiaonrek and Takoulgue were also subdued about this time or shortly before. When the overthrow of these various tribes left them nought to fear, the Iroquois plotted the destruction of the French colony of St. Mary's at Onondaga, and the destruction of the missionaries who had begun to labor in the various tribes, and the French escaped only by stratagem in 1658.

In 1655 the Mohawks renewed their treaty with the Dutch, who were threatened by the River Indians; and now firm in this support, renewed the war with the French and carried it on with vigor till 1667. At the same time they attacked the Abnakis who refused tribute, the Illinois and Dinondadies in the West, and the Susquehannas in the South.

Stuyvesant in 1662 proceeded with the Governor of Nova Scotia, and New England deputies to Albany, to obtain redress for the outrages committed in Maine, but the Mohawks were obstinate.

One Onondaga chieftain, Garacontié, labored earnestly for peace and the civilization of his countrymen, and effected a general peace between the Western Cantons and the French in 1665. The Mohawks and Oneidas held aloof, continuing their war against the French and their allies. Tracy, the French Governor, erected three forts on the Sorel to check their incursions, and sent De Courcelle to ravage the Mohawk towns; he did not indeed succeed, but his inroad in 1666 gave great alarm, and Tracy himself led another army into the Mohawk country which took Caughnawaga, Oct. 17, 1666. This produced a general peace, the French missionaries resumed their labors, and by the powerful aid of Garacontié who became a Christian, gained many from heathenism to the ennobling doctrines of the Gospel. This mission begun by Fremin lasted till 1685, and its results still remain in the three villages of Catholic Iroquois in Canada.

On the capture of New York by the English, a new policy was adopted by government. Nicolls protested feebly in 1666 against the invasion by De Courcelles of British territory, but the Iroquois were still really their own masters making peace with the French, war with Philip, war with Maryland and Virginia, Shawnee and Susquehanna. The war with the last named tribe began in 1661 and ended in 1675, with the overthrow of the nation, who became incorporated with their conquerors, forming a clan apart.

The war of the Mohawks with the Mohegans began soon after the commencement of the war between the western Cantons and the Susquehannas. On the 18th of August 1669, a Mohegan army attacked Caughnawaga, but it was relieved by the other towns, and the Mohawks pursued the Mohegans in their retreat. They subsequently attacked a Mohegan town, but were also repulsed : the government of New York then restored peace.

Meanwhile the missionaries, aided by Garacontié, were making considerable progress. His death, in 1675, was a severe blow to the missions. At this time, many of the Iroquois converts, and old Huron Christians in Iroquois towns, began to emigrate to Canada. Catharine Ganneaktena, an Erie, founded the village at Laprairie in 1668, which was soon visited by Garonhiague, or Hot Ashes, an Oneida chief, and Kryn, the Great Mohawk. Both settled there, the latter leading from Caughnawaga no less than fifty emigrants for conscience sake at one time. The village thus founded is now at Caughnawaga (C. E.) and St. Regis. A second grew up at the Mountain of Montreal, which is now at the Lake of the Two Mountains.

The Mohawks, after a battle with a portion of Philip's army, made a treaty with New England in 1677, and two years after with Maryland where roving braves had committed ravages.

France meanwhile was encircling the Iroquois territory. A fort rose at Cataracouy where Kingston now stands ; La Salle erected a block house at Niagara and a fort in Illinois. The energetic Dongan, Governor of New York, took alarm and resolved to drive the French north of the lakes. Under his impulse an army of 800 Iroquois marched in May 1683 against the Illinois, Miamis and Ottawas, the allies of France.

Their attack on Fort St. Louis led to a new war. De la Barre, the Governor of Canada, invaded New York with a large force, but after reaching Hungry Bay in 1684, patched up a sham peace, and made a precipitate retreat. The Iroquois had fearlessly awaited him, having just met in council the governors of New York and Virginia and New England deputies. After De la Barre's retreat, Dongan encouraged the Cantons to renew hostilities with the western French Indians, and made every effort to induce them to expel the missionaries. The treachery of Denonville, in seizing some Iroquois chiefs at Cataracouy in 1687 and sending them in chains to France, was however the finishing stroke. The Cantons expelled the missionaries and prepared for war with the French, as they were already at war with the Illinois, Miamis, Hurons and Ottawas.

Denonville, however, invaded the Seneca country with a large force of regulars, provincials, and Indians. The Senecas ambushed his path—a desperate fight ensued July 13, 1687, between them and the Indians in the French service, who finally, though with the loss of Ogeratarihen and Tageretonan, Iroquois chiefs, and Gonhiagui, the Dinondadie, forced the ambuscade. The Senecas then retreated and burned Gaensera, Totiakton and other towns, of all which the French took possession with all the forms of law. A fort was erected at Niagara as a check on the Indians. Though instructions from England prevented Dongan from pursuing his plans, an Iroquois army beleaguered Fort Frontenac, and a flotilla of canoes attacked an armed French vessel on Lake Ontario. Negotiations however ensued and peace was made at Montreal, June 15, 1688. The Indian allies of the French opposed peace, Abnakis attacked Mohawks at the Sorel, and almost at the Mohawk castles, the Caughnawagas took the field, Kondiaronk, the Dinondadie, by duplicity induced the Iroquois to believe the French merely plotting their ruin.

Andros and Leisler both urged the Cantons to action. A large force set out and on the 25th of Aug., 1689, surprised the village of Lachine by night, butchering on the spot, or by slow torture, two hundred of the wretched inhabitants.

War now existed between England and France, and the work of Dongan in assuring the Iroquois to the English cause, was producing its effect. After destroying Lachine, Leisler planned the capture of Fort Frontenac with an Iroquois force. But the vigorous Frontenac had just returned to Canada bringing back the captive chiefs, and offering to negotiate.

On their refusal he imitated the example so fatally set by Leisler. Lachine justified the use of Indians in destroying the English frontier towns. In February, 1690, Schenectady fell as Lachine had done. A terrible border war ensued. French envoys were seized at Onondaga, the frontiers were ravaged by hostile parties, an English Mohawk band under Schuyler advancing to Laprairie; but the principal operation was the advance of a large force of New York and Connecticut militia, and 1,300 Indians against Montreal, to coöperate with Phipps. Sickness broke out however, and four hundred Iroquois died in the camp. The defeat of Phipps completed the failure of the project.

The next year Schuyler again led his Indians to the very gates of the French camp at Lachine and in a well fought battle on August 11, 1691, killed St. Cyrque, the French commander, but was utterly routed by Valrennes on his homeward march. This and the ravages of Black Kettle, a great Onondaga chief, induced Frontenac to invade the Mohawk country, and on the 16th of February, 1693, he surprised the three towns of the tribe. A Jesuit, Milet, formerly a missionary now a prisoner at Oneida, labored to obtain peace, Tegannisorens, Garakontié II and Ourewaré did the same.

A series of councils and negotiations ensued at Onondaga, Albany and Montreal, and New England, New Jersey, New York and Canada alike sought to control the action of the League. As the Western Cantons continued the war, Frontenac, in 1696, advanced to Onondaga, which the natives burnt; and wasting that canton and Oneida he returned without meeting an enemy. Heavy losses in the west coming close on this induced the Iroquois to ask for peace, which was soon followed by the general peace of Ryswick (1697).

In this war, the first waged by the Cantons as English subjects, the Iroquois paid dearly for the privilege; in nine years their fighting men dwindled down from 2,800 to 1,300. They accordingly renewed their treaties with the English, but made new treaties with the French, and when the English renewed war maintained their neutrality, as did the Catholic Iroquois in Canada. After much exertion, a force joined Nicholson's expedition, but again the braves of the League perished by disease. Schuyler who had urged the step, now took five chiefs to England, and induced them to join Nicholson's (1711) expedition, a failure like the rest.

By the peace of Utrecht in 1713, France abandoned all claim to the Iroquois.

The warriors of the League then struck at Southern tribes, the Conoys, Tuteloes, and their kindred Tuscaroras, but when these last were overthrown by the English, gave them a refuge and a place as a sixth nation, yet without sachems. The Choctaws and Catawabas were next exposed to their murderous war parties.

The League was however declining, vices began to sap their strength, disease and war had weakened them, no new nations could be brought in as vassals. The French had endeavored to christianize them, the Dutch and English had hitherto done little. But about the time when Miller wrote, the matter was seriously taken up. The labors of Dellius had been but partial. Lord Bellomont, the successor of Fletcher, made great efforts to establish missions, the Society for Propagating the Gospel joined, but no mission was really established till 1705, when Rev. Bernard Freeman took up his residence at Schenectady. His labors were continued by Barclay, Van Driessan, and others, and an Episcopal Church formed in this canton.

The increase of English population drove many, however, to Canada, and others to the banks of the Ohio, where the Senecas and Shawnees formed a town, and where the remnant of the Susquehannas appear, under the name of Mingoes. Unprincipled traders and land speculators had so oppressed them, that when war broke out with France, in 1744, the six nations absolutely refused to take up arms, and it was not till Colden had employed promises and caresses, and Johnson his rising influence, that they took the field, but as on previous occasions, when they joined English expeditions, lost fearfully by smallpox. Some raids were made by the Caughnawagas from Canada, and by the Cantons into that province, but the Six Nations met severe losses, and in 1747, again resolved on neutrality. They indeed lost all British feeling, and the colony of New York began to dread them, while nevertheless it refused them justice. The Moravians, next to the Jesuits the most successful with the red men, at this very juncture offered to found missions, but the government would not adopt any plan for the civilization and due management of the Indian tribes.

Availing himself of the discontent, Picquet, a French priest, in 1749, established a new Christian village at Oswegatchie, now Ogdensburgh, and soon drew numbers from the Cantons. When war broke out, in 1754, Johnson induced the Mohawks to join the expedition against Crown Point. In the battle with Dieskau, they engaged their kindred Caughnawagas, losing Hendrick, their king or chief, and many of their bravest warriors. On this the Cantons again resumed their neutral ground, and did not again appear on the field, till 1759, when a thousand joined Johnson in the expedition against Niagara, and rendered essential service in the defeat of Aubry. A large body also attended Amherst the next year, but abandoned him after the fall of Fort Levi, as he checked their savage desires.

While the Cantons themselves had thus reluctantly acted in the war, the Canadian Iroquois of Sault St. Louis or Caughnawaga, the Lake of the Two Mountains and Oswegatchie were constantly in the field. All now passed under the British rule, and the Cantons saw how blindly they had acted. Their territory was now to be swept away by the increase of the British colonies. The Iroquois plotted the overthrow of the English, but Keashuta the Seneca lacked the requisites of a leader. When Pontiac divulged his scheme, Keashuta joined him. The Tuscaroras drove the traders from Fort Pitt and slaughtered them at Beaver Creek. The Senecas destroyed Fort Venango and every soul in it, then with the Delawares besieged Fort Pitt.

Sir William Johnson used constant effort to save the rest of the Cantons, and regain those in arms. In a council at Johnson Hall, in September, 1763, the eastern Cantons took up the hatchet against the Senecas and Tuscaroras. Yet at that very moment the Senecas were slaughtering the English train near Fort Schuyler. As Pontiac's power declined, Johnson's influence prevailed, and in April, 1764, the Six Nations made a treaty with him, which was confirmed in a national council at Niagara; Keashuta soon after submitted, and Pontiac's war closed by the treaty of Oswego in July 1766.

Two years after, the king or head chief of the Cherokees made at Onondaga a treaty of peace and friendship with the Six Nations.

In November, 1768, Johnson, in the treaty of Fort Stanwix, agreed with Tyorhansen of the Mohawks, Canaghagueson of the Oneidas, Seguareesera of the Tuscaroras, Otsinoghiyata of the Onondagas, Tegaca of the Cayugas and Guastrax of the Senecas, on a line beyond which the whites were not to encroach. This line started at the mouth of the Tennessee, ran along the Ohio to Kitanning, thence to the fork of the west branch of the Susquehanna, along that branch to Tiadaghton Creek, then to the east branch, following it to Owego, then to the Delaware, and finally to Wood Creek. All other lands were surrendered in consideration of the sum of £10,460 7s. 3d.

New England missionaries, especially Kirkland at Seneca, now attempted to convert the Cantons, and in 1770 the Society for the Propagation of the Gospel again attempted the work. The book of Common Prayer was reprinted. In Canada, Oswegatchie was abandoned and its people joined other villages, but the Tarbells, Groton boys, naturalized at Caughnawaga, finding themselves viewed with jealousy, had founded St. Regis in 1756.

In 1774, Cresap provoked the western Iroquois to war, and Logan, of the old Susquehanna tribe, retaliated with fearful vengeance, till his power was broken in the terrible and well fought battle of Point Pleasant.

When the American Colonists rose against the Home government, from whom the Cantons had received but favors, Johnson's dying effort was to bind the Cantons to the crown. All but the Oneidas, who were influenced by Kirkland, espoused the side of England during the revolution, and under Sir John Johnson and Colonel Guy Johnson, seconded by Brant, the real war chief of the Mohawks, proved a terrible scourge to the Americans. The Johnsons convened councils at Oswego—the Provisional government held a general congress at Albany, in August, 1775, the last in which the Cantons together treated with New York. But it failed to change the position they had taken. Strangely enough, the Americans succeeded better with the Caughnawagas, who positively refused to aid the English, and who, when Carleton threatened to deprive them of their land, laconically answered: *We have arms.* They subsequently even offered to send a body of warriors to Washington, but the hero was averse to employing Indians in the war, although Mohawks were actually in the field at St. Johns and at the Cedars against the Americans.

In 1777, it was formally announced that the council fire at Onondaga was extinguished. Brant led the Indians to the siege of Fort Schuyler, and to the battle of Oriskany, where the Mohawks especially suffered. Those in Burgoyne's army proved, however, of little service.

In December, 1777, Congress addressed the Cantons, as a last appeal for neutrality, but in vain. Johnson and Brant from Niagara, were hounding on the warriors to ravage the frontiers. In February, 1778, Lafayette held a council at Johnstown. There were few Mohawks or Cayugas, no Senecas. A treaty was made with the Oneidas and Tuscaroras, and proffered to the Onondagas.

In June, Brant defeated Captain Patrick; in July he cut to pieces a body of 50 militia; and made Wyoming a scene of slaughter never to be forgotten. Col. Butler, to chastise this, destroyed Unadilla and Oghkwaga, but Brant took vengeance in the slaughter of Cherry Valley, and peremptorily ordered the Oneidas to join him. The Onondagas fluctuated till Van Schaick marched against them. Then they openly took sides with the English and joined in the predatory war.

To check this, General Sullivan and Clinton in August, 1779, entered their territory, and defeating Brant at the Chemung, wasted their whole district, destroying Chemung and many other towns. All was now desolation, misery and ruin amid the fugitives who crowded around Niagara. Brant was however unbroken; he retaliated by invading Oneida, destroying the castle, church and dwellings; and followed up the blow by ravaging Harpersfield, Schoharie and Canajoharie.

Sir John Johnson, with a force of Tories and Indians amounting to 1550 men, soon after advanced to Schoharie, and after defeating an American detachment under Col. Brown, engaged Van Rensselaer, but was defeated in 1780. The peace left the Iroquois completely at the mercy of the Americans. All but the Oneidas and Tuscaroras resolved to emigrate, and the British government assigned, first, Quinté Bay to the Mohawks, and in 1784 a district on Grand River to all the Cantons. The American government, by the treaty of Fort Stanwix, October 22, 1784, confirmed the Oneidas and Tuscaroras in their possessions, guaranteeing to the others the lands in their actual occupation, on their ceding to the General government all west of a line beginning on Lake Ontario at the mouth of Oyonwayea Creek, then south to the mouth of Buffalo Creek, and thence to the north line of Pennsylvania, which it followed west and south to the Ohio. Brant was greatly opposed to this, and endeavored to form a great Indian union against the Americans, but the Iroquois made a new treaty with St. Clair, in 1789, at Fort Harmar, and gradually settled down to a state of peace.

When the western Indians, following Brant's plan, began war in 1790, Pickering negotiated another treaty with all the Cantons except the Mohawk, which renewed in 1794, settled all questions in controversy. New York meanwhile, in 1785 and 1788, purchased the lands of the Oneidas, Tuscaroras, Onondagas and Cayugas, except a reservation for each.

The last council with Pickering, in November, 1794, was attended by some of the greatest men of the League, Honayawus or Farmer's Brother, and Cornplanter or Gyantiwoha, who had both fought under Beaujeu, and Sagoyewatha or Red Jacket, the most eloquent Indian of his day.

From this time the various Cantons have ceded most of their lands. The Cayugas began in 1795, and dispersed, some joining the Senecas, some going to Grand River, and others to the west. The condition of peace led to some improvement. Brant among the Mohawks employed his time in translating the book of Common Prayer and part of the Bible, and till his death in 1807, labored for the real good of his countrymen. The Quakers, as early as 1796, began their civilizing labors among the Oneidas, and soon after among the Senecas. The Oneidas, already converted in part to Christianity, were rapidly becoming a civilized people. Among the heathen portion, who had now forgotten their ancient deities and worshiped only Hawen-niio, the Lord God of the Christians, arose the prophet Ganeodiyo, who produced a great reformation, especially in regard to the use of intoxicating liquors.

In 1803, the Rev. E. Holmes, a Baptist clergyman began a mission among the Tuscaroras; and in 1805, the Rev. Mr. Cram of the Evangelical Missionary Society of Massachusetts attempted to found a mission among the Senecas, but was repulsed by Red Jacket.

Tecumseh drew some Senecas to his standard, and in the war of 1812 the Canada Iroquois were very actively engaged, and rendered great service to the English cause. The American Indians at first sought neutrality, but took the field after a time, and the two sections of the League were thus carrying on the destruction of the nation. After the battle of Chippewa, both sides, however, laid down the hatchet.

Onondaga was deemed the centre and head of the League. Each tribe was divided into families, the Bear, Wolf, and Tortoise, with subordinate ones not uniform in all the tribes. Each of the families had certain hereditary sachemships. The sachems were the rulers of the nation. They succeeded in the female line, and the great sachem of Onondaga, the Atotarho or Sagochiendaguete, was the head of the League. No one could marry a person of the same family, even though of another tribe. The rules on this point were very minute. They adored originally, Aireskoi, or Tharonhiawagon, but learning the name Dieu, from the French, address God as Niio, which enters into the common form, Haweunii, God who art master. The worship of Aireskoi was by offerings of the flesh of animals, tobacco, and the like, and at times by human sacrifice. They honored also genii, or spirits, especially those of maize, pumpkins, and beans. Their worship had certain great feasts of the year, some, especially the Hononouaroia, marked by very strange rites.

They interred the dead temporarily, and about every tenth year, collected all the remains in one long grave, lined with furs, and containing kettles, arrows, and various articles. These are the bonepits occasionally met in excavations.

Prisoners were treated with great cruelty, forced to run the gauntlet, mutilated, and often burnt at the stake. The invention of this savage custom, and of scalping, was attributed by the Algonquins to the Iroquois. The dress of the men, was a mere breech cloth between the thighs, the ends hanging over a girdle, and that of the women, a short petticoat of furs, both wearing moccasons and leggins, and at times a mantle, and afterwards a blanket. Their houses were of bark, laid over a good frame like an arbor rounding on top. These houses were ranged in streets, and surrounded by a palisade, beyond which lay their fields.

Their numbers never, probably, since 1600, exceeded 15,000, if they ever reached that point, and are now about 9,000, which may safely be taken as their average population.

On the restoration of peace, the Rev. J. C. Crane founded, in 1817, a Seneca mission that still subsists, the tribe dividing into a Christian band, under Pollard, and a heathen band adhering to Red Jacket, who persisted in his hostility till his death in 1830, although his family had become Christians. The Methodists established and still continue a mission at Oneida.

In 1826 and 1839, the Senecas, or rather a few drunkards in their name, sold to the Ogden company all but the Tonawanda reservation, and the tribe lost 200,000 acres. This led to emigration. In 1840, 430 Oneidas and

500 Senecas removed to *Grand River*. Others at an earlier date, settled at Sandusky, and were subsequently removed by the General government, west of the Mississippi. In 1820, the Oneidas purchased a tract on Green Bay, and a party removed thither. Among these *Eleazer Williams*, subsequently the *soi distant* Louis XVII, labored as an Episcopal missionary.

A party of Senecas, Tuscaroras and Cayugas, about 1846, set out for the lands west of Missouri, were imposed upon, and nearly all perished. The survivors returned heart-broken to New York.

In 1849, the Senecas abandoned the old Sachem system and adopted a constitution with elective chiefs, and both sexes adopted more closely the dress of the whites. At the same time, the state authorized each tribe to divide the land held in common among the individuals or families. Provision was also made for schools and for the education of Indian teachers at the State Normal School.

The Catholic villages in Lower Canada have had an uneventful history. Caughnawaga, Aquasasne or St. Regis and Canasadaga or the Lake of the Two Mountains, are quiet villages, where the Indians live much like the whites around them, more indolent, but possessing churches, schools and council halls.

Note 30, *page* 68.

ARNOUT CORNELISSON VIELE, the Government interpreter, figures frequently in accounts of this time. He was taken prisoner in 1687, by Denonville, on his expedition against the Senecas, and came on bearing a letter to Gov. Dongan. Having sided with Leisler he lost his office under Fletcher, but was restored by Bellomont and rendered good service.

Note 31, *page* 69.

MR. MILLER's advice may seem strange, but its wisdom seems to have been admitted. The Bible has never been translated into any of the Iroquois dialects. In the commencement of the last century, the Rev. Mr. Freeman translated St. Matthew, a part of Genesis and Exodus, and a few Psalms. This was never printed; but in the *Mohawk Book of Common Prayer*, printed in New York, in 1715, Genesis I, II, III; Matthew, I (in part), II, V, and Psalms, I, XV, XXXII, appeared. The same parts of Genesis were reprinted with the prayer book at New York, in 1769. Not possessing a copy of the prayer book printed at Quebec in 1780, I can not say whether it contained any part of the Bible. St. Mark translated by Brant was printed with the Common Prayer, London, 1787, and reprinted at New York in 1829; St. John was printed at New York in 1818; St. Matthew in 1831; St. Luke in 1833; Acts and Romans and Galatians in 1835, and Isaiah in 1839.

In the other dialects no part of the Bible has been printed except St. Luke which appeared in Seneca in 1829.

Thus not only no Bible, but not even a Testament has ever been printed in any of the languages of the Five Nations, the rulers of central New York, although the Bible societies of New York have printed both in tongues of far distant nations. See Dr. O'Callaghan's *Catalogue of American Bibles*, pp. 26, 146, 201, 214, 228, 244-5, 263, and his History of the Translation of the Book of Common Prayer into the Mohawk Language, in the *Historical Magazine*, I, 14.

END.

www.ingramcontent.com/pod-product-compliance
Lightning Source LLC
Chambersburg PA
CBHW021939160426
43195CB00011B/1154